# BEYOND THE IVY LEAGUE:
## A Chosen Career Path

BY

PEARL CHASE

PEARL CHASE BOOKS

pearlchasebooks@gmail.com

Also by Pearl Chase

**FROM THE FARM TO HARVARD:**
*My Amazing Journey*

Copyright © 2012 Pearl Chase

All rights reserved.

ISBN: 0615606784

ISBN-13: 9780615606781

Published by Pearl Chase Books

All rights reserved, including internet rights, media rights, and the right to reproduce this book or portions thereof in any form whatsoever. Reserved rights do not include material from other authors quoted or summarized.

For information address Pearl Chase Books

pearlchasebooks@gmail.com

To God and to my family
whom I love dearly.

# Acknowledgments

The author wishes to acknowledge the invaluable assistance of the following people: Dorothy Chase and Karen Stabeno;

# FOREWORD

A career is what you make of it. It can take many twists and turns and have some ups and downs, but it is largely a matter of choice, preparation, energy, effort, and happenstance along the way that define what your life's work will be.

I am an educator by choice. I began as a secondary-education teacher. Along the way I prepared myself in my home State of Louisiana for teaching in higher education institutions. My preparation for research and administration in higher education was done in the Ivy League at Harvard University.

After graduation, I went beyond the Ivy League into colleges and universities to practice what had been preached to me. That's where I expended a lot of energy and effort to get where I wanted to be when I wanted to be there. I had goals. Of course I had certain expectations of my career beyond the Ivy League, but as happenstance would have it, others in the workplace had a lot to do with whether I achieved my goals. I must acknowledge upfront that I owe a huge debt of gratitude to the President of the first university where I was employed after graduate school. He mentored me and taught me administration in colleges and universities. I owe my career, in large part, to him and to his efforts on my behalf.

Here is how my career unfolded.

# CHAPTER 1:
## MY IVY LEAGUE EXPERIENCE AT HARVARD

My Ivy League experience was at Harvard during the 1980s. I entered the University's Graduate School of Education (HGSE) in search of a doctorate in Administration, Planning, and Social Policy. I actually received the master's and doctor's degrees before I left.

When I first got to Cambridge, I settled into a private room in the coeducational Cronkhite Graduate Center building and began to acquaint myself with the other graduate students. The accommodations were nice as were the graduate students I met. The staff of my building had made an attempt to introduce us by placing pictures and information about each of us on the walls. We looked like a miniature United Nations in session because of the multitude of nationalities present in our living quarters. Right away I knew I would learn almost as much from my living environment as I would from the professors in the classrooms. Some of the students that I became more than a passing acquaintance with were from Thailand, India, South Africa, Chile, Nepal, The Bahamas, Taiwan, and Ghana. Additionally, in our compact living environment there were more than thirty nationalities, and in the Graduate School of Education as a whole there were many more than thirty nationalities from foreign countries in addition to many ethnic groups from within the United States. This milieu provided many hours of fun, interesting conversation, and storytelling. You would be surprised at some of the things we talked about. Then again, maybe you wouldn't be. You could just imagine some of the things you could tell others about yourself, your family and community, your childhood, habits and customs, your high school and undergraduate education, dating, your dreams, successes and failures, career, and future goals along with some of the other things that helped to shape you into the talented, inquisitive, and engaging individual you are today. Imagine hearing those and other things from individuals whose background, culture, and customs, religion, political, and geophysical environments are foreign to you. It was eye opening, informative, and enjoyable to say the least. As you might imagine, there were as much common ground, as many common interests, common dreams and aspirations, and similarities among us as there were differences. Otherwise, how would we all have arrived at the same place with the same or similar goals in mind?

Almost all of the foreigners I talked with held a stellar view of Harvard that they were attending and the Ivy League in America in general that they were not attending. In their home countries, most of them said, attending America's Ivy League was a sure sign of high personal and academic achievement and a great predictor of future productivity and success. The name "Ivy League" meant something good in their countries just as it does in America. It connotes excellence and conjures up senior-level positions as if by magic even for careers that had become stagnant or frozen in mediocrity. All of a sudden, people and companies that once overlooked them demonstrated a new-found interest in their talent and potential as evidenced by the Harvard brand or the Ivy League mystique that their degrees portended. I was buoyed by their excitement and happy to hear their validation of my choice of graduate schools or, more accurately, of the graduate school that had chosen me out of so many applicants, especially since HGSE had an acceptance rate of approximately 10% of applicants worldwide. Now I could go on my way and feel good or at least 'not bad' about all of the money I would have to pay for my doctorate degree. I guess I should say pay back since I was on a free grant and the rest was student loans. I had little or no money to pay out-of-pocket as I attended Harvard. Anyway, I was beginning to feel that I was in a warm, nurturing, and welcoming environment in my living quarters among United States and foreign students. But, the welcoming did not end with my introduction to my fellow graduate students in our living quarters, the Cronkhite Graduate Center.

The efforts to welcome us were multifaceted. In addition to the Cronkhite Graduate Center's welcoming activities, the HGSE's Admission Office and Dean's Office hosted wine and cheese parties to break the ice and to assure us that each of us deserved to be admitted to Harvard. Evidently, years of experience had taught them that many students familiar with the Harvard brand and the Ivy League mystique came to the University still believing that their admission was all a big mistake or a fluke or that they were dreaming and would soon awake and discover that their being admitted to study at such a prestigious institution was all a cruel joke, a mirage that would soon evaporate into a nightmare. It didn't. Both the Admission Office staff and the Dean's Office staff could not have been more reassuring and gracious. By the time their planned activities were completed, we were beginning to feel very fortunate and important. Indeed, we were impressed with ourselves. Another nice, welcoming gesture was the number of currently enrolled students who came over to meet and greet us new students. This established camaraderie, a link to past years, and a bond of friendship among us that lasted the entire time we were in residence and, for some of us, even until the present time beyond the Ivy League and into our professional careers and our separate and personal lives. Having settled into my living quarters, it became time to branch out even more.

I began to acquaint myself with my surroundings at HGSE and in Cambridge, Massachusetts. HGSE is on Appian Way and it borders Radcliffe Yard and the Graduate School of Arts and Sciences. The main buildings are Longfellow Hall which is the administration building, Larsen Hall which is the classroom building, and Gutman Library which is the education library and the education-faculty office building. Just about everything we needed was in close proximity and so convenient. Also close around us were small department stores and restaurants, such as Crate and Barrel, Au Bon Pain, Yong and Yee Chinese Restaurant and many more shops and eateries. What I especially enjoyed exploring was the Harvard Coop which is a large department store and bookstore that contains clothing, shoes, jewelry, electronics, furniture, appliances, kitchenware, and almost anything one could want. Plus, listen to this, if you applied, the Harvard Coop automatically gave Harvard students a credit card. Isn't that great? I thought it was. Right away, I could see a Harvard tee shirt and other memorabilia in my future.

One cannot come to Harvard and not visit Harvard Yard, the site of the original Harvard College that began in 1636 as "New College." There is so much beauty and history wrapped up in that little section of land called the "Yard." The first things one notices are the many different and beautiful gates to the Yard, gates that have been added over the centuries and tell a story themselves with their fancy and ornate designs. These gates have admitted and released from the Yard many students who have become world leaders in politics, governments, arts, sciences, philanthropy, and law, along with Nobel Laureates, Pulitzer Prize winners, entertainers, educators, and public servants. Indeed, eight Presidents of the United States have been through those gates to graduate from the University. Harvard Yard is graced by a statue of John Harvard sitting in his captain's chair. John Harvard was the University's first benefactor who gave the College more than 400 books and half of his estate upon his death. The College's name was changed from New College to Harvard College in deference to his generosity. Holding a very significant place in the College's history is Massachusetts Hall, the oldest building still in use on the Yard. Massachusetts Hall was built around 1718 to 1720 and it houses the university President's office.

Inside Harvard Yard are quite a few buildings; however, none is more significant than Widener Library and Memorial Church which border Tercentenary Theater, the grassy center of the Yard and a very significant spot in the life of the university. It is the place where commencement exercises are held each year. Across the street from Harvard Yard is Harvard Square, which is not square but a rough triangular shape. It is a mixture of shops, restaurants, inns, small businesses, arts, cultural, and historical sites. As I walked through the Square in the 1980s, my path was often interrupted by break dancers spinning around on their heads and shoulders on flattened cardboard boxes they carried around in search of a convenient spot on the street to demonstrate their 'gift' of dance and 'slew' of performance and entertainment skills.

After familiarizing myself with the community I would call home for the next few years, the time came for me to register into my school, HGSE, and get busy with the activities that universally describe the life of a graduate student—studying and writing. Registration was easy, fast, well-organized, and somewhat different from what I had experienced at colleges and universities elsewhere. I am not familiar with the registration practices at the other Ivy League schools, but at Harvard I was introduced to the custom of "shopping week" in order to select my classes and complete my registration into HGSE.

Let me describe "shopping week" for those of you who are not familiar with the custom and want to know what it is. Shopping week is the first week of classes. During this week, students at the university as a whole are allowed to "shop" for classes by visiting classes in session at the school at Harvard that admitted them, at other schools at the university, and at the Massachusetts Institute of Technology (MIT), which is a short distance down the street from Harvard in Cambridge. We students were given a list of required courses and elective courses and told to visit for several days or the entire week any professor's class into which we were interested in enrolling. By visiting, we were able to see the professor's teaching style, course requirements, personality and charm or lack thereof. We could also determine if the professor and his or her requirements, style, and personality meshed with our level of commitment to the coursework, our own styles, personalities, abilities, and interests. On the surface, this was a good concept of academic matchmaking, and I soon discovered that I liked the practice very much. In addition to its registration purposes, it allowed us students to shop professors we had heard of before entering the university to see who they really were even if we did not want to take their classes. Professors benefited, too. For example, some professors had so many students shopping their classes until students filled the classroom seats while others stood along the walls of the rooms and yet others sat on the floor inside and outside of the room just to hear them teach for a day or two or a week. This probably gave the few professors who pulled in such huge crowds an ego rush for a few minutes initially. Then they probably just felt appreciated for their academic renown and their research, publication, and teaching acumen. Another benefit for these few professors with all of those interested students was the position they were in to select the students who would have the opportunity to study under them and have these professors' help in the shaping and mentoring of their academic and professional careers. These professors also had the ability to limit their class size, as did other professors, but they were able to do so with only the students they expressly chose as opposed to the students who chose the professor and his or her class.

To limit their class sizes, these professors usually assigned to students a three- to five-page paper on a given topic to be turned in the day before shopping week ended. After reading the papers, the professors would choose about fifteen students to enroll in their classes and then notified the lucky fifteen of their selection so they could put the class on their class-registration schedule. I was in one of those highly-visited classes of one of those highly-visible professors. When she made her assignment for selection purposes and I saw what it was, I eliminated myself to save her the trouble. After all, I had already satisfied my curiosity on who she was. I was one of many who was not serious enough about her class to write a five-page paper that soon into my studies. Write a five-page paper before I completed registration? Come on. Really. I immediately shopped an elective class that did not have the requirement of writing a paper two days into registration week and before I had a chance to do my research and put forth my best effort. So, do you see why I was enamored with the concept of "shopping week?" It worked for everyone—professors, students, and the registrar in the school's administrative team.

This is how the registrar and the administration benefited. We students completed our class schedule of required or core courses and elective courses, obtained our advisors' signatures, and filed the completed schedules in the registrar's office by 5:00 p.m. on the last day of shopping week. Once this was done, the need to add or drop a class and the recordkeeping and staff work to do so were all but eliminated. At least during my time in residence, I never heard of any student adding or dropping a course during the semester. Thus, all parties benefited from shopping week—students, faculty, staff, and administrators.

With registration over and done with, classes began in earnest during the second week of the semester. That was great. I was anxious to see what the Ivy League had to offer me or what it would do to me, whichever one proved appropriate in the coming months. Right away, I experienced what made up the Harvard brand that had been so renown and venerable for approximately 347 years when I entered. Among other things, the "brand" employs extremely rigorous admission practices that reject about 90% of applicants and yield some of the best students in the world. It offers cutting-edge research, an unsurpassed, excellently-prepared faculty that some would call superior. There was also adequate to excellent teaching and mentoring of students by some faculty. Some would call Harvard, its brand, the other Ivy League colleges and universities and their mystique arrogant and self-important. They may not be completely wrong in thinking, saying, or writing that, but I would ask this question, "How can these eight institutions of higher learning last from 140 plus years to more than 300 years and remain at or near the top in the United States and in the world if they were not doing something right to engender, prolong, and revel in such high reputations?"  People and organizations cannot fool or dupe the majority of people for 375 years in the case of Harvard the oldest Ivy to 146 years in the case of Cornell the youngest Ivy.  Two additional questions come to my mind on this subject.  First, "How could Ivy League institutions attract a large share of the brightest minds and continue to maintain their high standards and stellar reputations for 146 to 375 years if they were not doing something to attain and maintain those perceived standards and reputations?" The second question is, "Would not graduates reject the Ivies' claim of excellence in education and leadership in the world for up to 300 or more years if those statements or perceptions were unfounded?"

Anyway, when classes started we were totally immersed in our studies either in class or in libraries or in our rooms. I often joked to my family and some friends who asked me what was graduate school in the Ivies like? "It was like a pressure cooker," I would say. "They 'cook' you under high pressure at a really fast pace." Of course, I was semi-joking with my crude analogy, but the essence of my statement is true. The mystique of the eight Ivies is no mystery when it comes to academic studies. They provide highly-qualified faculty who walk in, teach, assign work and deadlines, and leave. We then scatter and get busy doing what we came to do in as cogent and thoughtful way as possible to meet those requirements and deadlines only to repeat the process in rapid-fire succession. We tried our best not to be eliminated by classmates who produced much-better-quality papers in a short time. You should see the heightened interest in what the other classmates earned on their papers when they were handed back. That's where the pressure came from more so than from the professors. No student there would dare admit that he or she could not do as well as another classmate. This brought on many late-night hours of study, research, writing, and rewriting. That's what I meant by 'cooking' you under high pressure. The fast pace is evident, too. Because they admit so few students and reject so many, the Ivy League prefers full-time graduate students overwhelmingly, and they do not allow you to camp out at the institutions. You cannot just enroll, take a few courses when you feel like it, or stop out for a semester or two and resume your studies at your leisure. Other applicants want their opportunities to be admitted to the very-limited, coveted slots for students. So, at Harvard in the Graduate School of Education, each student was required to take 16 graduate credit hours per semester, and complete all classroom coursework for the master's degree in two semesters or one year and for the doctor's degree in four semesters or two years. We did not have classes during the summer months. That's fast paced but certainly doable. I took 16 graduate hours the first semester and after that I took 20 graduate credit hours per semester. Get in and get out. That's the way to do it. In addition to the coursework, we, of course, were required to do the qualifying stage and the dissertation for the doctor's degree, but they did not carry separate graduate credit hours or classroom time beyond the in-class coursework hours we had already earned. The qualifying paper and dissertation just had to get done and we knew it and did it.

Usually in higher education in the United States, doctoral students are allowed seven years to complete their degrees. While technically we may have been allowed seven years at Harvard, the actual time that the university had us in residence was two years. We could complete the qualifying paper and either stay in the area or leave Cambridge and return to work while completing the dissertation. Thus, our doctorates took approximately 3.5 to 4 years, roughly half of the customarily allotted time of seven years.

As I mentioned previously, I majored in Administration, Planning, and Social Policy with a Management Concentration. I chose as a dissertation topic, <u>Black Women</u>

<u>College Presidents: Perceptions of their Major Job Roles, Problems, Expectations, and Experiences.</u> I chose this topic for two main reasons. First, there was a dearth of research in this area of the literature in higher education. In the mid-1980s, there were approximately sixteen black ("black" was the term at the time) women who were college presidents and little was known about them as a group. My dissertation was the first study I found on a group of black women college or university presidents. The second reason I chose this topic for my dissertation was because at that time I had hopes of joining that group or a similar group of women who had climbed the stairs to the number one spot and had become the chief administrator or chief executive officer at their respective institutions of higher education in the United States. All I had to do was complete my two years of coursework, pass my qualifying stage, then grab a job in a college or university, leave Cambridge, Massachusetts, and get busy working, learning, climbing that ladder, and completing my dissertation

while on the job. Two years after I left Cambridge, I had gained a great deal of management experience and had completed my dissertation. I returned to Harvard for Commencement. My graduating was a magnificent achievement of which my family and I were proud, and Commencement was a joyous and momentous occasion that I still remember fondly.

To share my culminating moment in the Ivy League, I invited a few friends and all of my family. Some of each came to Cambridge to share my happiness. In attendance were my mother, Rebecca, my sisters, Dorothy, Novia, Leca, and Sandra Faye, my brother, Robert, my brother-in-law, Rick, and my niece, Rebecca. They had a grand time going through the festivities of the day with me. Commencement itself is a grand, colorful, fun-filled, festive occasion. The activities are held annually in Tercentenary Theater, the large, wide, grassy area in Harvard Yard surrounded by dormitories and other buildings, most notably Widener Library and Memorial Church. Candidates for degrees from the College and the ten Graduate and Professional Schools gather together in black robes for bachelors and masters candidates and a choice of black or "Harvard Crimson" robes for doctoral candidates. Have you seen the Harvard Crimson robes? They are not the regular shade of crimson. Have you seen them in bright sunlight? Well, if you have not, you should go online and pull up a picture of a Harvard Commencement and check out the colorful sight of "Harvard Crimson" robes sprinkled among the black robes on degree candidates assembled in the sunlight in the outdoor Tercentenary Theater. It is a sight to behold!

The ceremonies are equally as colorful and interesting. The University President (who was Dr. Derek Curtis Bok during my time there) sits on a three-legged chair that dates back several centuries. Oh come now. It is not a four-legged chair with one leg missing due to age. It is made to be a three-legged chair. Another interesting tradition in the Commencement ceremonies that dates back to the 1700s is the inclusion of the sheriff of

Middlesex County, the home of Cambridge, Massachusetts. He is on stage wearing striped pants, a morning coat, a top hat, and carrying a staff. A loud voice calls out, "Sheriff, pray give us order." The sheriff approaches the microphone, bangs the stage three times with his staff, and says in a loud voice, "This meeting will be in order." This signals the opening of Commencement ceremonies, and the sheriff's proclamation never fails to elicit loud cheers and whistles from eager candidates for degrees. There is no way to curb the enthusiasm even with the sheriff present. It is just so unique, traditional, historical, and cute. The ceremonies continued with a combination of unique and commonplace activities, and I was anxiously awaiting the time for the Dean of the Graduate School of Education to approach the microphone and present us to the President by saying those famous and highly-anticipated words to the university President and the two governing boards. The words are, "Mr. President and Fellows of Harvard College, Mr. President and the Board of Overseers." While standing, we the degree candidates from HGSE cheered our

Dean heartily and turned our tassels on our mortar boards or hats after the President responded to our Dean and conferred the appropriate degree, master's or doctor's, on us. With that done, we sat down and candidates from another school stood as their dean approached the microphone. I was now an Ivy League graduate for the second and last time. I was a Harvard doctor. I had graduated from an institution that was 351 years old that year—an institution that was 140 years older than the United States of America. What a history and legacy!

Now all I needed to do after the conferring ceremonies was to walk across campus with the crowds as each group of graduates returned to its school location for the actual awarding of degrees followed by the meal with our families, friends, and invited guests.

As I reached Radcliffe Yard behind Longfellow Hall, the administration building for HGSE, I took a seat along with my friends and fellow graduates in the section reserved for us. When the awarding ceremony began,

I stood between two friends, held hands with one of them, and together we approached the stage with a slight tear and the widest grins we'd ever had. I gave my name to the assistant dean and watched as she located my degree, passed it ahead of me to the associate dean and dean on stage. As they shook my hand and said congratulations, I exited the stage to a bouquet of red roses my brother, Robert, had waiting for me. With the blessings of God, I had gotten in and out of school for the last time. After lunch with family and friends under the HGSE tent, it was time for the Afternoon Exercises with the Commencement Speaker to begin in Tercentenary Theater. For my master's graduation, our speaker had been His Majesty the King, Juan Carlos of Spain. The Speaker for my doctoral graduation was His Excellency, Richard Von Weizacker, President of West Germany.

When everything was over and I realized that I was leaving Cambridge for good and even if I returned the same people I knew would not be there, I started reminiscing about some out-of-class activities and conversations that were both memorable and defining, showing us that who we were becoming in our growing process was not much different from who we were and had been in the past. While I was thinking, my mind rested and rehearsed a conversation some others and I had with one of our classmates who had been gathering information to write a book after graduate school. Henry was his name. He was quiet and shy, but brilliant and accomplished. At times he would look at me as if he did not know what to make of me from head to toe. You see, one minute I was as quiet as he; the next minute I was as talkative as a parrot. Sometimes I got on my soapbox and went on and on about things that mattered a lot to me or that had had a deep impact on my life, or that had affected in some serious way those who were near and dear to me. Included in this category were my quiet and gentle mother and all of the elderly relatives who had long since departed this world. My dad, on the other hand, was much more of a talker and character than my mother and for that reason I did not feel as protective of his feelings as I did mother's feelings.

Anyway, one day Henry asked a group of us who was sitting around the dinner table at Cronkhite Center, "Who is your favorite President?" That day, to Henry's surprise, I put on my "soapbox" hat, and not knowing which Pearl I would be he just went along with the flow. To Henry's surprise, I answered, "My favorite President is Lyndon Baines Johnson, LBJ." (This was in 1984 before there was a President Barack Obama.) With his fork halfway to his mouth, Henry asked in a high-pitched voice, "Why?" "I mean …. I thought your answer would be different." "Why so?" I asked. To this he humped his shoulders and smiled shyly. I think he expected me to say President John F. Kennedy, JFK. That would not have been a bad answer because I certainly do admire JFK. Indeed, most black Americans or African-Americans admire the Kennedys and the Clintons—Bill and Hilary.

Then I began to explain my choice and perspective to Henry. "The executive orders issued by LBJ are hard to beat, in my opinion," I told him. You see, I grew up as a poor, black girl in the Deep South where cotton is king and segregation in everything was the ongoing theme and prevailing way of life. In the Jim Crow South, with its segregation, we blacks had separate entrances to buildings, separate water fountains, toilet facilities, restaurant use, schools, neighborhoods, and separate just about everything. Separate was not as bad as the "not equal" part. Blacks in the South, at least the ones I knew, were not just clamoring to be with whites. The fact that things were not equal was the problem. When put into practice, separate as we knew it, was inherently "unequal" and self-perpetuating for generations past, for the present, and for generations to come. There were no "integrity" police to initiate and maintain separate but equal, and we were powerless to make things better because we had no voice or influence because we had no control over resources, processes, and procedures, no right to hold office, and no right to vote in elections.

Basic human rights were not afforded many of us, and human dignity was accorded only a few of us, if any. Only low wages and tedious, menial labor were lavishly heaped on us and "denial" was the name of the game for almost anything from the basic to the superfluous. Discrimination and intimidation were the tools of choice to accomplish these diabolical goals. During the civil-rights era of the 1960s, things began to change under the leadership of civil-rights advocates and President John F. Kennedy, but when he and Martin Luther King, Jr. were assassinated, hearts were broken, hopes were dashed, fears were rampant, and doubts were recaptured. Ears were attuned to hear and eyes were opened to see what the new President, Lyndon Baines Johnson, would do. Would things move forward or would the South revert to its old, familiar habits? To our great surprise, LBJ issued executive order upon executive order and set in motion the social, political, economic, and historical gains and rights for blacks and other minorities that were unprecedented prior to his administration.

Things that began with JFK actually were accomplished under LBJ for me, my parents and siblings, my peers, and my fellow black Americans. President Johnson had chosen to move the clock forward in blacks' favor rather than back to the old status quo and desperate gloom for a large segment of this nation's people. It must be noted and said that when things that are right are done regardless of for whose immediate relief and benefit they are done, the entire nation will ultimately benefit. And so it was for the United States of America. The country accorded rights, privileges, respect, and dignity to the long disenfranchised in this country and received the loyalty, respect, contributions, and gratitude of a segment of the population who had contributed beforehand under slavery, extreme duress, and hostile political, social, and economic climates. What should they get for their contributions and trouble? Why, of course, what others have—rights, privileges, respect, dignity, self-worth, worthwhile pursuits, and fulfilled dreams and promises. Varying portions of these rights, privileges, and attributes came with LBJ's executive orders and the right to vote in elections.

I must say that my proudest moments during this period were not for me but for my parents and grandparents who had never voted in their lives. You would have been proud, too, unless you have a very hard heart. You should have seen the way they and others in our little rural community went in droves to register to vote. When an election day came around, my parents dressed up in their Sunday best clothes and went to the polls, followed the process sometimes grudgingly told to them, and finally voted for their choice to lead or represent the city, state, or nation. It was an experience like no other that they had had in their lives—one that did not come easily in that some people had died trying to procure those rights. It was an experience that they did not take lightly then or now. Excitement, pride, and self-worth exuded from their faces. "Thank You, God" emanating from a grateful heart rolled off their tongues and through their lips, and a smile like no other I had seen on them graced Mother and Daddy's faces when they returned home that first voting day and the kids who were home asked them, "How was it?"

With the courage it took to initiate and complete the process, they recounted the story and how they felt, whom they had voted for and why, and what they hoped their candidate would do and be like if elected. Hearing this unfamiliar conversation, we kids just laughed and laughed and felt like our mama and daddy were really somebody special and important, as if they had played a game and, after a hard-fought contest, been declared the winners. There was no turning back. My grandmother, my mother and father, and my aunt who lived to be 100 years and 6 months always voted in *each* local, state, or national election. They never missed, and they often rode together on those days.

When I finally got off my soapbox in response to my classmate Henry's provocative and interesting question, others at the dinner table had the names of their favorite President and stories to match. There were classmates from different states and regions of the United States which brought about different life experiences. There were also different ethnic groups from within the U.S., and classmates from other countries who had comments and questions of their own. Needless to say that was an interesting evening meal. In fact, most of our evening meals were interesting and informative with topics ranging from the mundane to the provocative, from the day's activities to solutions to world events and crises—that is, if we were in charge or at least in positions of influence.

After dinner and conversation ended that evening, some of us went downstairs to the basement to watch a presentation and slideshow from a Malaysian classmate who wanted us to explore in pictures and stories life with its ups and downs, successes and failures, beauty and squalor in his country. Others of us went down the hall to the red Reading Room to read newspapers and magazines from around the world, or to our own rooms to study, or to libraries. At Harvard, as with so many other universities, learning and growth experiences are always taking place, and at any given time one is hard pressed to tell whether more of it is in the classroom or in the environment.

Sometimes we grow through structured classroom learning opportunities. At other times we are fed and we grow and are challenged by our own actions, inactions, and reactions, by our thoughts and intentions, and by our assumptions and realities, especially those assumptions that become our realities.

Take for example the case of a crying South African classmate named Emma. Emma received a scholarship from Harvard, an organization in her country, or perhaps both to study for a Master's degree in Education. Since arriving in Boston/Cambridge, Massachusetts, she had busied herself with enjoying many new experiences among them avid photography and snow activities. Since she was seeing snow up close and personal for the first time, she combined the two activities to take and send home to her family many, many photographs of the city and of herself making snow angels in that big, wool coat that she wore even when the weather did not seem to warrant it. By all standards and appearances, Emma was smart, talented, and happy. Two of her strong suits were expressing herself well in writing and smiling constantly as she passed by you on campus.

So, it came as a surprise one day when Emma approached me at the dinner table with a face full of freely-flowing tears. We were always friendly with each other, though we seldom shared a table. That evening she came over and wanted the chair next to me. The occupant, seeing her distressed state, obliged her willingly, asking in the process what was wrong and could she help. "No," was Emma's short answer as she took her seat. Her emotional state was not lost on several people who were at the same table and at other nearby tables. Three or four people left their tables and dinner plates to come over and offer her their sympathy or empathy and primarily to eradicate their curiosity about the scenario playing out before their eyes. They joined the people at our table in asking, "What's wrong, Emma?" "Can I help?"

Emma's tears increased and she said, "I just want to talk to Pearl."

I immediately felt proud and eager to help and, at the same time, clueless and powerless to help. I, too, wanted to know what was wrong and how best to help fix it. Emma just put her hand on my arm, held her face in her other hand, and continued to shed tears. She shook her head in response to any questions from others.

So I said, "We can talk when you are ready." To this she nodded.

The commotion was not lost on two of my favorite people—Janet from Australia, the student assistant director of our residence center, and Rob, a Caucasian American, an all-around good guy, and everybody's friend. Janet did not approach Emma at the time and I don't know what she thought, but she took action. The next morning, Emma woke to a dozen, long-stem, gorgeous red roses at her door and a note that said, "I don't know what's wrong, but whatever it is I hope these make it all better."

Rob, on the other hand, came to the table that next morning and assumed that apartheid games were being played with Emma on her part-time job. He asked someone else where she worked since Emma was not at the table. When he found out, Rob announced that he was going to pay her jobsite a visit and asked two other guys to accompany him. They were going to look around, and see how she was being treated all in an effort to right a perceived and assumed wrong, show her friendship, make her comfortable, put the fear of God (or at least the administration) in her boss, and fight any vestiges or reminders of apartheid that might have reared its head toward her in the U.S.A. After breakfast and knowing no more than the previous evening, Rob and crew set out like Don Quixote on the trail of some assumed mischief.

Emma, to my knowledge, still had not told anyone what was wrong. She certainly had not told me. Rob, meaning well as always, sat at the jobsite and observed, then went in and talked to her boss in generalities to run interference and head off any thoughts he may have had of abusing Emma in language or actions. Later during the week, Rob sent others to periodically and anonymously watch her, her coworkers, and boss and report to him anything untoward. His assumption became his reality in that Emma never told any of us why she had been crying. But, since we all knew she was from South Africa, it was easy for some classmates to reach into their minds and into the pages of world history and draw conclusions, fashion actions and reactions, and assume things real or unreal—all for a noble purpose. Afraid of even a hint of what was known to be in her background finding its way into her present situation, Rob and a few others bent over backwards to make her feel cared for and welcome. No sir, No ma'am none of that funny stuff toward Emma, especially with all of her classmates around.

About a week later when everything was back to normal and Emma's tears were all but forgotten, she came to tell me the problem. It seems that her boyfriend who was studying at a university in Colorado had come to visit her that weekend to tell her that their relationship was over and he was getting married to someone he met in Colorado. Emma said that she couldn't talk to any of us then, and in light of everything that her classmates had done for her, she did not know what to say to her friends now. "Well now," I looked up beside her head and said, "Is that it? That's what this was all about?" I didn't have the heart either to tell Janet or Rob and his crew about the real culprit they should have been pursuing. It would somehow cheapen their efforts. So much for the gallantry, assumptions, heroics, noble efforts, and social consciousness of Emma's friends and classmates who demonstrated concern and protectiveness and did what they could to right a perceived, assumed wrong in order to help her. To this day, I bet (and hope) they still feel good and are telling their children about how they came to the aid of a crying South African at Harvard.

So much for my thoughts as I was walking back across campus from the Afternoon Exercises on Commencement day. I had many happy memories of my experiences at the university, but I decided to discontinue my thoughts and join in the conversations around me.  As the day ended, my family, friends, and I relaxed and enjoyed our time together, and later I began to think in earnest of life beyond the Ivy League.  I began thinking of my chosen career path that awaited me.  The main vehicle to my career in higher education administration that I had taken was an Administrative Fellowship through the Woodrow Wilson Foundation. My life as a student was over.  Hello, Woodrow Wilson Fellowship.  Hello, my position as a university administrator.

# Chapter 2:
## Woodrow Wilson Fellowship

The time came for me to go beyond the Ivy League and choose a career path. Consequently, I left Harvard and began my administrative career in higher education. I had completed all coursework for the doctor's degree in Administration, Planning, and Social Policy, so I left with only the dissertation needed to complete my degree requirements. Now I had to find a suitable job. This was no small task since I did not want to start at or near the bottom and work my way up the administrative ladder nor did I want to work in just any state or region of the country.

Two classmates of mine had accepted positions as "assistant to" a university president and a vice president where they bypassed the laborious challenge of starting in lower positions and working day and night for an opportunity to be noticed and promoted. Additionally, by being an "assistant to" they had the opportunity to see the big picture of how a university operated or how a major unit of a university functioned. They had aspirations, as did I, of being the president/chancellor, or executive vice president/provost, or vice president/vice chancellor of a university or a system of colleges. But, my next challenge and opportunity was how best to get the attention of a college/university President who had an open "assistant to" position and was willing to hire me.

I consulted the *Chronicle of Higher Education* which lists most open positions in U.S. colleges and universities. I found several promising leads in different regions of the country and proceeded to prepare application packets. Before I could mail them, I stumbled upon the Woodrow Wilson Administrative Fellows program when a representative of that organization came to campus for a visit. My life began to change immediately. I soon discovered that the most attractive and expedient way for me to begin my administrative career was through a fellowship, and the Woodrow Wilson Foundation representative was there staring me in the face with a welcoming smile and an outstretched hand to shake. Problem solved. Why had I not thought of that sooner?

Of course I had to apply and get the fellowship. That involved competition, but I was competitive. In fact, I felt ready and able to tackle anyone, any issue, anything to get where I wanted to be. All I needed was the right institution, a little orientation, a little time to get up to speed, and a little mentoring from a higher up in the organization. I thought that if others had received their formal education and training and had gone on to become cogent and effective leaders and topnotch administrators, certainly with a little on-the-job training I would find myself in this elite group of senior-level administrators and managers. Here I was just jumping and prancing to get my opportunity. Had I not been trained by some of the greatest minds, researchers, practitioners, and leaders in the education, administration, and managerial fields? Why sure.

According to the Woodrow Wilson Foundation's website, the Woodrow Wilson Teaching Internships and Administrative Internships started in the late 1960s and early 1970s as a program to allow young graduates to teach or assist in the management of Historically Black Colleges and Universities (HBCUs). Over the years, the Foundation has selected and awarded fellowships to more than 21,000 leaders in education, the arts, sciences, government entities, and nonprofit organizations. Today, 14 Nobel Laureates, 35 MacArthur Fellows, 14 Pulitzer Prize winners, and many, many government leaders and college presidents have been Woodrow Wilson Fellows.

I might point out that in the Ivy League, the current Presidents of Harvard and of Yale have both been Woodrow Wilson Fellows. Also former Presidents of Cornell University, the University of Pennsylvania, and Princeton University have been Woodrow Wilson Fellows at some time during their educational and career paths.

I am proud to say that in 1985, I became interested in the Woodrow Wilson Fellowship Program, and the end result was that I was selected as a Woodrow Wilson Administrative Fellow. I was now a member of that august group of leaders who bear the name "Woodrow Wilson Fellow." Here is more of how it happened for me.

As I mentioned, a Woodrow Wilson Foundation recruiter came to the Harvard Graduate School of Education campus and I had a first interview with him. I was impressed with what he had to offer and he seemed impressed enough with me to recommend me for the second round of interviews that were held in New York City. I left Boston/Cambridge for the Big Apple already feeling good about myself and the prospects of being selected by the committee that would interview me. I went in with a smile and left with a smile. They were seated around the large conference table with stacks of papers in front of each person. No doubt this was information about each candidate and letters of recommendations. They looked me over, introduced themselves, and nodded as I introduced myself. I was a tad bit nervous, so I took the opportunity to locate the friendliest, calmest looking face so that I could focus on him when I answered the questions they were going to ask me. The gentleman who asked the first question looked at his sheet and then at me and said "on one of your letters of recommendations from Harvard, someone said that when you speak, everyone listens. What did they mean by that?"

All of my recommendations were from Harvard faculty or staff. So I answered, "If you tell me who said it, I can tell you what he or she meant."

Thus, the very first question and response called for a short break for them to huddle. After a very short discussion, the gentleman who asked the question responded that the committee was not at liberty to divulge names or sources on letters of recommendations. They then went on to the next question, looking a little disappointed that I did not venture an answer for the very first question that they had been dying to ask me.

It did not escape me that a Foundation that chooses and places Fellows at institutions across the U.S. would want their Fellows to be respected and respectful, listened to and listening, supported and supportive. But most of all, if they are told that everyone listens when a certain graduate student speaks, according to that letter of recommendation from Harvard, certainly the Woodrow Wilson Foundation would think that this person would represent them well and be an influential asset to a university president and his programs, goals, and staff. I began to peak in confidence and I tried not to disappoint them in my answers to subsequent questions. Evidently I did well. When it was over, they smiled and I left smiling. I felt good all the way back to Boston/Cambridge.

I told some of my friends when I returned that I thought I had done well in the interview and it seemed to me from the occasional nods and the looks on the faces of some of the committee members that they were pleased enough with me to select me as one of their Administrative Fellows. They did. Within ten days I heard from them. They informed me of my acceptance and of my next assignment, which was to interview with some Historically Black Colleges and Universities (HBCU) to find a suitable match for my skills and interest and those of the university that chose to hire me. The Woodrow Wilson Foundation would pay all expenses for the interviews and provide additional supportive services to me and the HBCU that hired me. Great.

Most HBCUs are in the South and I am a Southerner so that was a good fit for me. The recruiter who had come to HGSE contacted me to make arrangements, and I started interviewing with several colleges right away. My interviews were enlightening but not all encompassing. The presidents and staff members told me some things about the goals and priorities of their institutions with subtle glimpses of internal politics and struggles. I interviewed at two institutions. The two interviews I took also gave me an idea of what I would be doing or expected to participate in if I were selected to join the institutions. The position at the first college was called Assistant to the President. At the second institution, it was called Executive Assistant to the President.

The first college in which I interviewed conducted two interviews on the same day for the same vacant position, and unbeknownst to me selected the other candidate for the position the same day while promising me a second interview. The President of the college never gave me a second interview nor did he ever send me a rejection letter to this day. I discovered that the second interviewee had been hired when an HGSE classmate of mine who had friends working at the institution called one of them and was told that the college had indeed hired a new Assistant to the President that very week, and he was to begin work immediately.

I felt a little dejected, rejected, and insulted. Why would a college president just string me along like that without being upfront, courteous, and professional? The choice of whom to hire was certainly his. He didn't owe me anything except perhaps professional courtesy, closure, and a written response to my failed efforts at employment at his institution. I began to wonder if he was this lackadaisical, whimsical, unconventional, unpredictable, and unprofessional in his management style with other more serious aspects of the college and with those who were already employed there. Did he just arbitrarily leave loose ends? Or did he simply forget? He even may have thought that I would know that I would not be joining the institution if I had not heard from him in a reasonable amount of time after the interview. Okay, so I'm making excuses for him now.

I assumed then, but I know now, that college presidents are very busy people. All of the constituencies of the college are constantly bidding for and demanding a piece of his or her time and attention even if they don't come to his or her office. Faculty, staff, and residential students (especially residential students) are always doing things that will ultimately require the president's attention.

That is why a good and effective president surrounds himself or herself with ample and qualified staff in his or her office to help perform tasks ranging from the mundane to the extraordinarily important. Search committees, if used, are often the vehicle to handling properly applicants and candidates for positions and following up with information, closure, and professional courtesy. So, it seems a simple thing to say "yes" or "no" in writing to a candidate for a job.

Enough of that. Let me tell you more about the first interview itself. I'm no expert on interviewing etiquette and technique, but I thought it a little quirky or strange that the president interviewed me while standing behind his desk the entire time. At no time did he sit, smile, or take the time to follow up on a response that I had made to one of his questions. The other candidate had interviewed before my scheduled time, I discovered later on. I should have known by the President's behavior that something was awry and deep down inside of me I did, but I sat there, plowed through the interview question after question, and put my best foot forward. Never once did I act on my suspicion or show him disrespect.

One revealing question he asked me during the interview was about how I thought I would be at doing statistical reports and whether the Graduate School of Education at Harvard had prepared me for that. Some schools of education did not do so, he noted. I assured him that the Harvard Graduate School of Education had done an excellent job of preparing me and other graduates to do and handle well whatever situations presented themselves in higher education institutions. That's one of its main functions—its reason for being. It is superb at accomplishing its goal of training leaders in k-12, higher education, research, and policy and practice in education. I told him that I liked to do reports and that while I was not a statistics major, I did have a bachelor's degree in Liberal Studies (Mathematics) and a master's degree in Mathematics Education and I believed that I would be a good choice for the job because I could do with numbers what the President needed done. As I said this, I did note in the back of my mind his reference and concern about what schools of education, in general, teach. He, on the other hand, had a master's of public administration from the Harvard Kennedy School of Government, but was President of an institution of higher education. I didn't have to wonder very long at who he thought might be out of place in an educational institution—I who was about to become a doctor of educational administration or him and others like him who had master's degrees in public administration. The job of Assistant to the President was offered to the first candidate who was interviewing that day—a young man with a master's in public administration from Harvard's Kennedy School of Government, the same degree the President had. Oh well. Do you see why my antennae sprang up during that interview? Do you know why any president of a higher educational institution should question the legitimacy and fit of an administrative degree from a school of education for use in an institution of higher education? I am telling you all of this because I want you to know that when you leave graduate school behind (even the Ivy League behind), you will meet all kinds of leaders and decision makers out there who have many perceptions and opinions founded or unfounded.

I had no such problem with the President of the second university where I interviewed. He, too, was an Ivy League graduate and not from a school of education. He seemed genuinely interested in what was best for the university he headed. Several of the first things he told me during the interview were that he believed in a strong work ethic, and that there was absolutely nothing he would not do for the good of the university. No kind of work or task at the university was beneath him, he said. I liked his sincerity and stated dedication, and it was one of the things that made me want to become a part of the university. He asked me other questions regarding issues in higher education—questions that I cannot remember specifically at this time. But, I do remember a question about how I rated myself on background and experience in higher education administration, to which I responded that my background and experience was teaching in secondary schools and a little at the university level. Regarding administration, my experience was the proverbial mile wide and an inch deep. It consisted of formal study and training as a graduate student at one of the best schools of education in the U.S. and in the world, but the actual experience was limited to student work in the offices there and internships. The President smiled broadly at the honesty of my answer and lack of inflation of my experience level and probably thought to himself that this is someone he could mold and mentor to his particular style, especially if he were to hire me as his Executive Assistant. I had not been shaped to any particular management style or viewpoint on leadership issues. My knowledge was theoretical and imbedded in the ideal, the novice, and cutting edge innovations that hardly held their own when confronted with the realities of actual personality, human behavior, financial and budgetary constraints, governance, student, community, managerial, and leadership issues that presented themselves daily in the workplace. A gradual dose of reality was all that I or any other wide-eyed, idealistic, and new doctoral graduate needed to serve as a springboard that would catapult us to our career achievements in college or university administration. And while I sat there, I wondered if I would become a college or university president and how long would it take me. Not long, I concluded, if I connected with the right institution, with the right people, and had the right attitude, goals, drive, and mentoring. I felt that I was ready as I would ever be. The President of the second institution must have felt so, too. Within days after the interview and my return to Boston/Cambridge, he gave me a formal offer of hire in writing with salary specified and start date determined, and I accepted hire.

When I got to the university, I found his statements to be true. I noted the 'sparkling' appearance of the campus and the buildings. There was a complete lack of litter or paper or trash on the campus or in any of the buildings. This took extra effort and dedication on the part of the facilities staff because of the number of students, faculty, and staff on that campus. It also pointed to the fact that the President himself treated the campus and facilities as if they were special to him. I vowed to do my best for the university in ways that I could.

In my mind, I thought about the two college campuses in their outward appearances and the impressions they made on me. The first campus was neat, but everything seemed uptight and smug as if there were too many things going on beneath the surface. It did not appear open and aboveboard. It did, however, have a great reputation for academic excellence, and it was located in a city and state that I have always wanted to explore and live in. The city was rich in history and had a reputation for supporting a desirable lifestyle. I need not tell you that four or more years of living as a broke graduate student will start anyone thinking of a lucrative job, roomy and affordable housing in a nice neighborhood, and a comfortable lifestyle. I was very familiar with the taste and versatility of Ramen Noodles, and my taste buds had long since desired a different diet and culinary experience. These were just a few of the things I would quickly change with my newly-found status of employed and salaried Dr. Chase rather than graduate student Pearl.

Another thing I noted about the two institutions was the proximity to other educational institutions. Within a thirty-minute drive or less there were other colleges or universities with a cohort of professionals, graduate students, and undergraduates pursuing their crafts and goals. I was sure that I would feel at home in any one of these universities' libraries. Remember, I still had to complete my dissertation. All in all, I felt that I was in a good place to start my career, and that I would learn, grow, contribute, and be mentored and shaped in my job at my new university. Things were looking up for me.

In addition, the Woodrow Wilson Foundation supported me in my position. The Fellowship Program Director kept in contact. He came to visit my President and me at the university and met with us separately. He, of course, did this for all Woodrow Wilson Fellows on the campuses where they had been hired. In addition to campus visits, the Foundation arranged for all of us Administrative Fellows to meet in the same location for a two- or three-day seminar once or twice a year. This was refreshing and eye opening in that the venues were in nice places, such as Atlanta, Birmingham, Las Vegas, New Orleans, New York City, Washington, D.C., and other interesting places. Additionally, during the seminars, the Director had a program planned for us with interesting information useful to us in our positions, keynote speakers, very nice dinners together, and other relevant activities. What was very informative were the sessions where each Fellow had the opportunity to share some things about his or her institution, job title, work assignments, experiences, successes, and disappointments at the colleges or universities. Sometimes these sessions generated very candid and honest comments about the institutions' achievements, culture, interactions, and relationships and how the Fellows felt about the institutions, their work assignments, and supervisors. I tried to be positive and for the most part my experiences at the university were positive ones and my growth and learning curve in higher education administration were measurable and immense. I liked my job and I liked being a Woodrow Wilson Fellow. I felt fortunate that my first experience beyond the Ivy League was satisfying, positive, and beneficial.

I was paired with a President who worked diligently and spent a lot of time, energy, and focus on ensuring that others worked equally as hard and effectively for the programs of the university. This was no small task because he demanded a level of excellence that was difficult for some to achieve. Indeed, some were simply indifferent or unwilling to cooperate to their fullest potential. I might point out that this is not at all uncommon in higher education or in any job market. Some employees are talented and do excellent work and are supportive of their supervisors. They buy into the agenda and work diligently for the success of their departments, while others want the job and accept the position without accepting the total package of supervisor, agenda, work ethic, project completion, and pride in achieving goals and advancing the department, company, or university as a whole. And yet again, there are managers and bosses on the job who should not be anyone's supervisor. They do not know how to communicate with people, how to manage fairly, nor what employees want or need in the workplace. There are many reasons for all of these situations, some of which I will delve into later.

But before I get ahead of myself, let me take the time to tell you something about my first job beyond the Ivy League.

# CHAPTER 3:

## My First Administrative Job: Executive Assistant to the President

My first administrative job beyond the Ivy League was Executive Assistant to the President of a University. I had been approved to write my dissertation on <u>Black Women College Presidents: Perceptions of their Major Job Roles, Problems, Expectations, and Experiences.</u> So you see, it was good that I was going to be an Executive Assistant to the President of a University so that I could experience and learn as much as I could about the presidency while I wrote my dissertation. Learn I did. I could not have had a better job title for writing my dissertation and very importantly for gaining high-level, relevant administrative experience for my future career in higher education administration.

I had heard that the President was scholarly, smart, energetic, hardworking, thorough, and detailed-oriented with a penchant for good results, a reputation for toughness, and a bit of a temper. Nothing got by him, they said. This made me a little anxious and scared about how I would relate to him and his office staff and a little curious and apprehensive about what plans he had for my role in his office and at the university. I did not want to be at odds with anyone, especially him, my immediate supervisor.

When I arrived the first day, I was assigned an office between the President's Administrative Assistant and the General Counsel. Every kind of supplies imaginable was on my desk and in the drawers. They had thought of everything that I could possibly need to do the great work that I was destined to do from the way everything looked. I noticed that I did not have a computer in my office. When I began to ask about getting one, the President's Administrative Assistant pointed

## My First Administrative Job:

at the two ladies sitting outside of the office door and said, "One of them is your secretary and the other is the General Counsel's secretary." Hello! Welcome to the world of a university administrator. I now had my first professional position in higher education and a secretary to match. My graduate student days were over.

I settled in, picked up the *Chronicle of Higher Education* that was on my desk and almost tossed it in the trash. I had my position. Knowing that it is much more than the classified section, I thought twice about it and started flipping through it and reading articles to keep abreast of issues in colleges and universities across the U.S. Then I busied myself arranging my office and putting away supplies and before I knew it lunch time had arrived. I didn't know anyone to lunch with and I didn't feel hungry, so I just stayed in the office, worked on my set up activities, drank a coke, and completed other tasks until it was time to leave for the day.

The next day, I found that I had been copied on several memos and a stack of other things such as a job description, reports, and a policy manual had been put on my desk. I familiarized myself with these along with a few of the Vice Presidents and other staff who stopped by to say hello throughout the day. Things were off to a gradual and good start. I hoped they stayed that way. I made a mental note to myself to stay abreast of names and faces and away from politics and hot topics that I caught a glimpse of in a few of the memos I had been copied on. I wanted things to continue going well and I wanted to make a good impression on my first assignment whatever and whenever it was. I didn't have to wait long—three days to be exact. My first assignment was to deliver the already-prepared speech for the President at the university's Opening Convocation for the Fall Semester. The President had a very important appointment out of town that could not be cancelled. My delivering the opening speech for him was his way of introducing me to the faculty and staff of the university. After a little bout of nervousness, I calmed down and got through it quite well, I thought. At least I didn't stutter all the way through the speech or turn and run from the stage before they introduced me. Since I knew no one there, I selected a fixed point straight down the center of the audience and I would first look straight at that point, then I would look left and next right of that point to cover the whole audience. It worked for me. I didn't notice any frowns, eye rolling, or bored looks. They seemed genuinely interested in me and my delivery skills and a little interested in what I said. I figured correctly as did the President, of course, that they would try to form an opinion and reach a conclusion about the President's new Executive Assistant right away. In the back of my mind, I hoped that it was a positive one and that I would be well received. I wanted my presence at the university to engender cooperation and support from the various constituencies on campus. I especially wanted the reports that got back to the President to be positive so that I would be off to a good start with him. After all, that was the main person that I had to please when all was said and done.

When the speech was over, several people came to the stage to greet me and ask me questions about my background. One person wanted a copy of the speech. I chatted with the first two or three people and told the other gentleman that he would have to contact the President's secretary or administrative assistant for a copy of the speech. Then I returned to my office, thanking God that I had passed my first assignment—my introduction to the university.

When the President returned, he gave me my second assignment. I was to become his representative to the university's faculty senate and attend all of their meetings. This I did immediately, and I was happy, innocent, naive, and unsuspecting until I got to their first meeting. Once there, my ears began to tingle with words and statements about him that were not complimentary or laudable. Could it be that some of these people did not like this highly-qualified, Ivy-educated, detailed-oriented, hardworking, energetic, spirited President? Was that what I was hearing? Were they not pleased with him and his administration of the university? Did they not feel included in the management and decision-making processes? Was his management style caustic as they were saying? Did I hear them correctly that they were going to evaluate the President and send the results to his bosses on the governing board, and to area newspapers in order to politicize the process and get the board and community to see things their way and act on it? Yes, no doubt about it that's what I was hearing. At that point, I realized that the President had told me absolutely nothing about the faculty senate to shape or bias my viewpoint of them and their activities. He just gave me my assignment. I was free to see things, form an opinion, conclude things favorably toward him or unfavorably, and act on my own personal and professional judgment. I did. I decided to take out paper and pen and make some notes about what was happening and what might be immediately down the road for the President. It never occurred to me that the President might already know these people. I just wanted him as one person to know what this group and the faculty they represented were planning to do to him. I wanted to help him. I was new at this and new at the university, and it didn't seem like a fair fight—all of them versus one of him. I was troubled about the fact that many of their stated complaints should not have been complaints. What they wanted to do was not for the faculty or a faculty senate to do, based on my limited knowledge of university management. They seemed to want to make decisions about administrative tasks that should have fallen to the President, Vice Presidents, and other administrative staff members. The primary responsibility of the faculty is to teach students and do research and have some input in decisions that affect them, their departments, and their academic freedom. From what they were complaining about, they wanted to manage the university on a larger scale. Even I knew that was not under the purview of the faculty or its senate. That was troubling, but I was especially troubled by the elation and glee in the room when they announced their decision to evaluate the President (negatively, I presumed), and send the information to his bosses on the governing board, and to the area newspapers.

Well, I did inform the President. He listened, but did not comment good or bad to me about the faculty senate. I continued going to senate meetings and giving the President a summary of what occurred. He never told me to give him a report nor did he say not to do so. I considered him wise to be aware and watch his comments and with time I came to realize how politically savvy he actually was. Each day, I became more and more cognizant of the institution's culture and the many stated and unstated dynamics in operation around the presidency in general, this President in particular, all the people who worked closely with him, and all of those who worked diligently against him. I began to see how very important it is to manage the politics in an organization while you are doing the nuts-and-bolts work of the university. When either slips, you find more trouble and chaos than you want or need.

Boy was I on a fast learning curve. Here it was two or three weeks from my arrival on campus and already I was becoming a bit but silent player in the drama that was university administration and constituency interactions. I almost said interference—Freudian slip, that's all. I was learning how to develop my own opinions about matters as they unfolded, because I was not encouraged, informed, or pressured to take any viewpoint or anybody's side, nor was I ever asked by the faculty senate or the President what I thought about viewpoints, actions, or reactions to anything that occurred on the campus. Was this entrenchment? Was it stoic and staunch self-confidence on either of their parts, or a wait-and-see what she thinks, or more likely an it-does-not-matter-what-she-thinks-or-does attitude on both of their parts? I did, however, notice an objection to me taking notes in senate meetings. But, for the most part, I just did what I wanted to do—what felt comfortable for me to do. I thought what I wanted to think. I had my mind made up on the viewpoints and issues, but I did not express it. It came as a surprise when I discovered that what I had concluded most of the time agreed or meshed with the President's way of thinking on all matters when he stated his viewpoints or objections about things. I, of course, never expressed my viewpoint or opinions—that is, in the early days, months, and years of my stay at the university. But, you know, things change and change they did. I came under attack by a constituency group of the university. That warranted a statement or two from me.

Anyway, to make a long story short, the faculty senate did evaluate the President. As expected, their evaluation was not especially positive or complimentary. They did send it to the governing board and area newspapers. However, it did not accomplish the results they had hoped it would. The President remained President, and the senate continued being the senate. Both continued doing what they were authorized to do and what they did best. This was new to me then, but not now. I am way past being surprised at what happens good or bad on college and university campuses. From my present vantage point, I must say that I am very pleased that this was one of my first experiences in university governance and management. I like that I was sent "cold turkey" into the environment that I wanted to be a rising star in, and I especially like that I was not told a course of action to take or what to think or what to do. I had some autonomy as a young professional, and I liked that. I was allowed to "feel" my way through situations and the environment, form and explore my own opinions and course of actions, and most importantly my new boss, the President, had the opportunity to see who I was, how I thought, and how I would react and grow as a young professional in higher education administration.

One enjoyable thing about being Executive Assistant to the President of a university was that the scope and range of duties, viewpoints, and vantage points were broad and all-encompassing. The job allowed me to see what the President of the university saw without my doing all that the President did, without my supervising the President's senior-level staff, and without my being responsible for what the President was responsible for. It was a position that gave me a broad view of administration at the top of the hierarchy, and a position that taught me a lot about administration in higher education. It was the single most important position for preparing me for what happens on a day-to-day basis at a college or university. It helped to prepare me for managing one unit of the university later on, but nothing beats seeing and knowing first-hand how all of the units interact, affect, and culminate in the whole work product of the university. Everything important in academic affairs, business affairs, financial affairs, student affairs, institutional research, advancement and development, facilities, and other areas of the university ultimately finds its way to the President's office.

How did this impact me? Well, when the receptionist logged in the mail, she brought it to my office. Therefore, one of my important assignments was to receive, read, and review all of the mail that came into the President's office prior to the President seeing it. This enabled me to know what was happening in every unit and department at the university in addition to knowing what was happening with federal, state, local entities, and individuals outside of the university who had business dealings with the university. After reviewing the mail, I then drafted a response to all of the pieces that I was able to reply to and sent the mail and my proposed reply or response to the President's desk for his review and action. Occasionally he used the response I drafted with additions or amendments. Sometimes he discarded my drafts in favor of his own response to a situation. I was never presumptuous enough to write a response to the President's mail and send it out without his knowledge or approval. My work was to assist the President in any way that I could and not act as President under any circumstance or overstep my boundary. Another responsibility I had with the mail was to proofread and review all grants, reports, and other projects that people and departments within the institution prepared to be sent from the campus to any federal, state or local government organization. This was in addition to the President's review and not instead of. After both of our reviews, if changes or corrections were needed, the grant or report or project would be sent back to the responsible parties and departments at the university for revisions or additional input prior to resubmission for the President's signature and submission to an outside agency. This was a lot of detail work, but it was very, very important in that what is sent out from an institution reflects on the institution in a major way, has a bearing on how the institution is perceived, and affects the amount of funds the university receives from agencies and organizations.

Another responsibility I had with the President was attending with him all meetings of the university's governing board. The President, based on his position, was secretary of the governing board. Therefore, as the President's Executive Assistant, I assisted with logistics and matters concerning the board, and wrote the official minutes of each meeting for the university President and governing board President's signature. Working with the governing board was an eye opener in the sometimes strange dynamic and political nature of the executive and administrative duties of the President and policymaking, governance, and oversight duties of the board. On quite a few occasions, discussions were spirited and sometimes contentious. It appeared to me that the board often delved a little too deeply into matters that were in the domain of the presidency and not the governing board. I don't want you to think I am all pro-President, but that is what I truly thought as I listened to them talk as I took notes. A few board members seemed to want to confuse the lines separating the two sets of responsibilities—theirs and the President's. I would sit, quietly of course, taking notes and watching with heightened interest the back and forth exchanges and conversations between two or more board members and sometimes between a board member and the President. This was a one in a thousand chance to see the board in action prior to an individual becoming President himself or herself. I must point out that very few people have the opportunity to work that closely with a governing board each month when they are not the sitting President of a university. It is good training especially for ambitious educators and administrators who envision a presidency of their own down the road someday. It is not good to walk into these situations cold-turkey or with rose-colored lenses. I say this because some of what I saw in action was not written in the books that one could study, nor was it what a naïve aspiring President might suspect. Some board members were relatively quiet while I could have sworn that one or two of them seemed to want to be the paid President rather than the unpaid board member, and I mean that literally. If I remember correctly, on at least one or two occasions the issue of a board member covertly coveting the President's job was raised and that question was put to a board member in a straight-forward manner in hopes of uncovering motives for some actions or proposed actions of certain governing board members. While watching the President and board at work and performing my ancillary duties, little did I know that later on in my tenure at the university in a different position, I would become the subject of much of their discussions and deliberations.

Indeed, I was a hot topic for a while. Keep reading. I'll tell you about it later on.

As Executive Assistant to the President, I was also a member of the President's Cabinet. The President's Cabinet consisted of all of the Vice Presidents, the General Counsel, and me the Executive Assistant. We met regularly to discuss and take actions on all of the actionable items from each unit of the university that was listed on the President's agenda for the meetings. In these meetings, we had open discussions and the President set deadlines for projects and stated how each unit was to provide input or expertise, if needed, for the completion of projects by the stated deadlines. Everyone was responsible for all of the departments within his unit, and quite often chairpersons and deans in the academic unit were summoned by the President or Academic Vice President to appear for a specified time at the cabinet meeting for discussions concerning their departments. In the same manner, mid-level department managers of non-academic departments were also summoned for a brief period of time. These mid-level managers included the Registrar, Financial Aid Office Director, Housing Director, Comptroller or Bursar, and other directors or managers. What was not resolved in the meetings was worked on until completion. The work got done. I participated in the work, but the General Counsel and I were staff in the President's suite of offices. We did not supervise a separate staff as did the other cabinet members. My job description had me supervising the staff in the President's office, but of course they already knew quite well what to do and they were actually supervised by the Administrative Assistant. They had been doing it for years before I arrived. Regarding the President's Cabinet, about the only thing I will take credit for doing single-handedly is stopping the Vice Presidents from smoking cigarettes incessantly in our meetings. This was before smoke-free buildings became the norm. I can't stand cigarette smoke. It stops me from breathing freely. After our meeting was over one day, I went to the offices of the smoking Vice Presidents and petitioned them kindly to discontinue smoking in the conference room during our meetings in that it was just not healthy for me and I couldn't take it much longer. It took me about ten minutes to get a consensus and accomplish this feat once I was thoroughly fed up with choking on smoke. Of course some of them just looked at me and grunted. You see, some people really, really love to smoke. But from then on they never smoked again in our meetings. So, what do you think about my anti-smoking stand? Did I earn my day's pay on that one or is that too insignificant to mention? Oh well, not everything I did was breaking new ground, digging ditches, or erecting bridges. As I said, I participated in all of the work, but I did not substitute for the President or supervise the Vice Presidents' staff as Executive Assistant, not to mention the fact that I was in a fast-paced, on-the-job, learning-while-contributing phase. There was nothing about their work that a novice Executive Assistant could supervise. The opposite was probably true of them. But, of course, I was not about to allow the Vice Presidents to supervise me. Only the President did.

## My First Administrative Job:

A clear picture of the financial management and condition of the institution is necessary and valuable for an administrator in higher education, especially for one who had hopes of climbing to the top position somewhere, sometime later. I received the overall picture of our university when I was Executive Assistant to the President. After I had been at the university for at least six months, I asked the President to allow me to have a complete printout binder of all accounts at the university. This was the same printout binder that the President, Vice President for Business Affairs, and the Bursar or Comptroller received each month showing the status and everything pertinent about all accounts at the university. With this information, I could monitor all accounts and determine when a department or a manager was close to depleting his or her funds or when they had spent too many funds too soon in the fiscal year and needed to be warned about going over their approved budget. It was good experience for me and good for managers too knowing that they had double even triple accountability and checks and balances watching to see that they managed their fiscal responsibilities well.

I especially benefited from the campus-wide budget hearings that the President conducted once a year when the new annual budget was being finalized. Each account manager was given a set of guidelines and parameters in order to submit his or her budget request for the new fiscal year to his or her department head. The department head reviewed and or revised the account managers' budget requests and sent all of this information up the chain until it passed through chairperson, dean or manager and eventually to the Vice President for that unit. The Vice Presidents of each unit reviewed, revised, and compiled and sent the budget to the President and Vice President for Business Affairs. Within a week, the President scheduled budget hearings with each Vice President and his or her unit managers for those items that represented new programs or significant budget increases. When one department or unit left, another came in, but I as Executive Assistant to the President

MY FIRST ADMINISTRATIVE JOB:

was with the President through the entire process. After the hearings were concluded, the annual budget was finalized and I had a good frame of reference for future use down the road in my career.

The President and governing board sometimes made new policies or revised existing policies. Once these had been approved and adopted, my responsibility was to revise, distribute, and maintain the University Policy Manual.

I also spent some time serving as a host to candidates who were interviewing for jobs at the University and working with the logistics of getting them about campus for their interviews. Frequently a group of us would be required to take them to lunch and see them to the airport.

The above were just some of my major duties as Executive Assistant to the President. Many things I did were things that are routine day-to-day administrative tasks. Having found a good measure of success in my position, I spent some time thinking about the employees at the university, what they wanted, and how best we could provide an environment that was conducive to good morale, teaching, and generating a good work product at the university. Years later, as I am writing this book, I decided to do some thinking about the topic of what employees want. I found that to be a perplexing and major issue that was never fully understood or resolved at the university where I worked, and that accounted for the majority of the stress, drama, dissatisfaction, and upheaval on campuses across the United States. What follows is some of what I think on the issue.

# Chapter 4:
## What Do They Want?

Quite often in colleges and universities the various constituencies have different viewpoints on how the institution should be managed, who does what, and what goods and services each individual or group could or should provide. I found this to be true of the university where I worked. Sometimes the variations in viewpoints produced stress, strife, and contention that took an effect on the morale of the institution and its employees. This is true of almost all institutions and organizations and is not unique to our university. Once low morale permeates the culture of the organization or university, it grows, matures, and reproduces itself sometimes slowly, sometimes rapidly but it stays around and has a negative effect on almost everyone and everything the organization or university does. New people who, in the interview process, seemed excited to come aboard are almost always drawn into the prevailing culture and morale of the institution in a very short span of time. Those of us who are supervisors, managers, senior-level administrators, and the President are often at a loss as to how to turn the situation around. A frequent and puzzling question is, how do we preserve what is good in the institution and protect the reputation and perception of the institution in the eyes of newcomers and the general public? The most confusing and commonly asked question from employers is, "What do staff members want?" Employees, too, ask a similar question, "What does my boss want from me?"

Let's look at the employee point of view first and see what they say about what employees want.

As can be expected, employees want many things and those things vary from institution to institution, group to group, and time to time. It could be easy to conclude that employees themselves do not always know what they want in that there is no one thing that satisfies everyone, and what satisfies in the short turn may not satisfy in the long run.

Take, for example, good pay, money, compensation. That is sure to be high up on the list of employees' wants and needs. There are few, if any, employees who don't want to be paid well for their services. Being compensated poorly, fairly, well, or highly will cause employees to look at themselves that way or conclude that that is the way the institution looks at them, values, or devalues them and their services. Thus, compensation affects morale, perceived status, contributions, performance, and loyalty of employees. Some poorly paid employees leave for more lucrative positions. Others, who are not as fortunate, stay on the job and just do enough to get by. They take the often unstated attitude of, "I gave as good as I got," when confronted about their contributions or poor performance. So, if you are a manager out there and you have someone who is offering lackluster performance and subpar contributions despite having the ability to do better work, take the time to examine his or her motivation, attitude, and compensation to determine if one is influencing or causing the other. Many people just do not want to do "free" work or take on responsibilities for which they are not or will not eventually be paid. Some will try to take on additional work to impress the boss in order to get a good evaluation or a promotion. But if those are not forthcoming, seldom will an employee generate extensive, uncompensated output for an indefinite period of time.

Money is high on the list, but it is not the only thing that employees want. I don't know of any employee who does not want to be respected on the job in addition to being compensated or rewarded for his or her services. If money sweetens the pot, disrespect sours the soup. Respect can be shown in myriad ways. How one is spoken to or communicated with throughout the day, the kinds of responses and feedback and individual gets to opinions, questions, or comments made, the type of projects that an employee gets, the committees to which he or she is assigned, office space, accommodations, fairness, or favoritism present in the environment, and other factors demonstrate the level of respect in the environment and the respect accorded an individual employee.

Problems occur in the institution or organization when people who work feel as if they are expendable and their feelings are not even respected. If they do not have a certain job title or management responsibility, some may feel that they are viewed as less valuable and their work is not appreciated, just used. If employees feel used and disrespected, they become less dedicated, less productive, less genuine, and less loyal. People start blaming others, shooting memos throughout the organization, and finding ways to align themselves with power brokers in the organization to get respect, protection, and appreciation in any way they can. In other words, employees start disrespecting the job and the workplace itself. Decision-making is delayed, nonexistent, or prolonged to the point of decision by acclamation and not by the responsible parties. With a little respect given comes respect returned, dedication to purpose, good camaraderie, and loyalty.

Other things that employees want in the organization or institution are meaningful purpose and achievable goals either stated or in writing. It is helpful for employees to know and managers to say why a certain project is being assigned and what its impact might be in the institution. Sometimes a federal or state grant could be at stake and dependent on a successful completion of a competitive project of which the employee is a part. If I were told of the potential impact of a project or assignment, I am certain that I would do the utmost to cross my t's and dot my i's, and I would take extra pride in the accuracy, thoroughness, and timeliness of my piece of the entire project.

Having clear purpose and goals are two very important desires that employees have in order for them to take ownership in their work and do their part as if the entire project depended on them and their contributions.

## What Do They Want?

I believe that there are very few people who start a job and do not want to be proud of what they do. The challenge is capturing those good intentions at the onset and maintaining the momentum or a good share of it throughout the employee's stay at the institution.

Employees also want good leadership from their managers. They want a boss who is knowledgeable about the department he or she heads and not just knowledgeable about office politics and kissing up to his or her higher ups in the organization to get ahead. Few people like working for a boss who can seldom offer guidance, input, ideas, or technical support to a project. Employees can grow and develop their skills in a department with a capable leader.

One of the objectives that an employee has is to build his or her career qualifications in order to advance at the same organization or take a higher rung on the ladder at another organization. Mobility is the key to career building and that cannot happen effectively if one is stuck behind a poor leader or is forever training an unknowledgeable, but politically savvy boss.

Employees want to know that the institution is there for them. They want job security, good benefits, and vacation time with pay. With the current economic climate and employment market, job security is rare. In past years, many people were accustomed to keeping their jobs and seldom being downsized provided their performance was adequate and the company's budget was intact. But now many employees are left to question whether they will be able to feed their families and maintain a desirable lifestyle. Job security based on the present-day economic climate is a very scarce commodity.

But, some employees worry about the security of their jobs even when the budget is sufficient. They are those who find themselves at the whim of unscrupulous bosses who do not value the merits, opinions, and contributions of those who are under his or her supervision. Let's face it, there are many workplaces and job requirements that are fine if only an employee did not work for an unscrupulous, crooked boss.

For those employees who feel that there is a bad fit between them and their immediate supervisor, the best thing to do is seek a different assignment within the institution if at all possible and if a public feud has not taken place to hinder and employee's prospects of finding a new, neutral, and supportive manager. This kind of move can have its advantages. It can decrease stress immediately, head off a demotion, dismissal, or further abuse in either direction, and bring on a new set of skills for a different set of duties. If an internal transfer does not work, then the employee should seek employment outside of the institution. He or she should try to obtain a new job before losing the present job in that it is easier to find a job when you have a job.

Unfortunately, many people who are dissatisfied with several or more elements of the job do not want to leave nor do they seek to leave. "Why should I leave?" some of them think, "I'll only mess up my retirement or benefits, or I might find a similar or worse situation elsewhere." Rather than leave, they want their supervisor or the President or Chief Executive Officer to leave. These disgruntled employees choose to remain in the environment and fight against their managers or against perceived wrongs. Staying may not be right or wrong, and exiting the environment may not be a good thing for them to do in an economic decline. The way the employees choose to handle the situation with the environment or management is something that needs to be carefully thought out and done in a controlled manner.

Unnecessary chaos and strife benefit no one in the workplace. Game-playing, stress, and one-upmanship can be more destructive to morale and a professional environment than anyone intended, except perhaps a sociopath. Once these tactics are put into play, they take on a life of their own and are difficult to halt. They result in prolonged poor communication, distrust, disloyalty, disrespect, dissatisfaction, disruption, and disorganization. Efforts to gain and maintain job security become distorted and in jeopardy, all of the things an employee and employee do not want.

All kinds of fallout can result from a dysfunctional environment when employees find themselves in a fight for job security. The organizational chart becomes a relic on paper. Managers can even attempt to set up their own little kingdoms on the job where they do not cooperate with other units or share information without coercion. This hurts the work of the institution or organization in that knowledge is power and information is king. By hoarding or strategically withholding key knowledge and information, some employees and managers think they can make themselves invaluable for a time and enhance their job security. Not all organizations function this way, but some do to a greater or lesser degree. It is certainly not a tactic that I would advocate.

Several concessions that employees want seem to be going by the wayside in the current job market and economic climate. They are good benefits and paid vacation time.

Employees are especially wary of working a job that does not pay benefits or decrease benefits such as health insurance for employee and family, 401k match, company retirement plan, and ample time off with pay each year. To avoid paying some of these customary benefits, some organizations and institutions are more and more hiring part-time employees or adjunct faculty who work less than the forty hours a week for fulltime status. However, with high unemployment rates, shrinking budgets, and downsized staffs, some employees accept the jobs with limited or no benefits or paid vacations and other disadvantages.

Now that we have taken a look at what employees want in the workplace, it is equally important to take a brief look at what employers want from the people they hire and the staff they maintain.

Qualified, competent employees top the list of items that employers and managers want in their existing employees and new hires. They want people who can enter the workplace and contribute individually and work

## What Do They Want?

in teams to get the job done. They also want employees who perform well over the entire term of their employment and not be just a flash in the pan.

Employers want good work ethic and teamwork. It is good for employees to be knowledgeable on the job, but it is even better to have good, solid performance of assigned duties and good productivity on shared work and goals of the organization. Employers want people to buy into the goals of the organization as evidenced by their work product and people skills.

Honesty and loyalty are also important to managers. Having trustworthy employees who give an honest day's work each day without constant oversight and supervision and are loyal to their departments, managers, and the goals and objectives of the institution are keys to success in the institution. They are what employers want from their employees.

Knowing what to expect as an employee and what employees would ultimately want from me as a manager, I accepted my first position where I was a manager or one of the managers of a unit of the university where I worked. I now had staff to supervise along with the Vice President of the unit. I was ready and on my way as the new Associate Vice President for Academic Affairs.

# CHAPTER 5:

## ASSOCIATE VICE PRESIDENT OF ACADEMIC AFFAIRS

Thinking about the workplace from the employees' points of view and the employer's, boss, or manager's points of view caused me to look at my own style, circumstances, and responsibilities as an employee as well as a mid-level and senior-level manager.

The career path I had chosen in college and university administration was one that would place me and keep me in a senior-level position that I hoped would lead to the presidency, if I were fortunate enough to attain that status. Putting forth good effort, doing well the individual work I was assigned to do, and working together with others when teamwork was required are all tasks that I had to do consistently in order to progress in my chosen career path. In my own personal assessment, I was much better at doing the individual projects assigned to me than I was at anything else in the workplace. At least I enjoyed those projects much, much more than I enjoyed anything else. I knew then and I know now that that could not be the totality of an administrator's job. So, I did all aspects of the job fairly well to very well.

As an employee, I was mostly satisfied. I had adequate-to-good pay, benefits, paid vacation time, excellent office space, very good and clear job duties, support for my career goals, a good mentor, opportunity to grow in skills and administrative abilities, and access to resources at the university. I had yet to grow and develop as a manager or supervisor in that I did not supervise or have line authority over other employees while I was Executive Assistant to the President. Those of us who aspire to be leaders and senior-level administrators in colleges and universities need experience in more than one area of the university and experience in supervising and managing a unit of the university. I didn't have to worry about this long because another growth opportunity quickly presented itself in my next position.

Having served as Executive Assistant to the President, my next position was Associate Vice President for Academic Affairs (Administration). In this position, I reported to the Vice President for Academic Affairs and had primary responsibility for the unit's budget along with projects related to non-tenure-track, tenure-track, and tenured faculty. I also did compensation and salary analysis and comparisons and other administrative reports and duties common to an academic unit. It was a position that allowed me to do what I enjoyed most and did best—reports and projects.

Making and administering the budget of a unit is very important in that the University received public funds; therefore, accountability was very high on the list of must dos for everyone from the staff member who oversaw a budget to the department manager, to the unit manager, and ultimately to the

President. At times I found myself questioning item by item things that were put in budget requests, wondering if they were important to have or pertinent to doing a good job.

The deans of the various departments reported directly to the Vice President and not through me. That was fine with me. It freed me up to do my individual work and help in other areas on an as-needed basis. Often I did not attend departmental meetings with the Vice President and deans in favor of doing the administrative work in the unit. While I did enjoy making and administering the budget and the other work, I did, however, miss some of the perks that came from working in the President's office, such as a designated parking space, a huge, nicely furnished office in a polished suite, an air of importance on the campus, a budget that was not strained or did not deplete before the end of the fiscal year, and a general overview of activities in all units. These were just a few of the perks I missed by leaving behind my old unit at the university.

## Associate Vice President of Academic Affairs

I don't want to sound paranoid, but one of the feelings I had in academic affairs, a feeling which may have been real or imagined, was that I was not viewed as a bona-fide member of the unit because of suspicion that my interests and loyalties were still in the President's office and that somehow anything that was said or done in my presence was automatically deposited in the President's ears and office. This was not completely true nor was it completely false. There have been many occasions when employees went to the President to explain themselves or their actions that I had observed about which the President knew nothing from me. That was always a source of amusement for me. Of course, the President would never volunteer this lack of information from me on the subject of which they were purging themselves nor would the President show through body language or eye contact whether the matter was known or unknown, significant or insignificant to him. He always listened attentively to what anyone said to him. On these occasions, I realized that the very presence of any current or former employee from the President's suite of offices in specific places on campus or in meetings and gatherings was a catalyst for catharsis later on for many employees whose actions or even ideas toward the President or the university were suspected of disloyalty, treachery, or, God forbid, treason.

I did not sense this purging process being made to the Academic Vice President when I was his Associate Vice President. Maybe it happened and I just did not know it was occurring. Or, maybe it was that managing in the academic unit lacked the flavor and broadness that it had in the executive office suite. Whatever the reason, it seemed strange in that, to me, most of the tension and discord on campus to this point in my career came from faculty in the academic unit and not from non-teaching staff in other units and departments on campus. My guess is that their energy and venom were directed toward the campus' highest administrator and not to the Academic Vice President who supervised them. They most likely viewed the Academic Vice President as a comrade or at least not the ultimate decision-maker and thereby not the "bear" to fight off if he did not agree with their viewpoints and ideas on decision-making and managing the university.

I liked working in the academic affairs unit because, in my mind, it embodies the main focus of a university—teaching, learning, and research. All of the other units of a college or university are important in their own way, but are ancillary and supportive of this main unit and main function of a university. At least that's how I view it, and I doubt that I will change that viewpoint.

My stay in academic affairs went smoothly until I was tapped to be Acting Vice President for Student Affairs at the same university. I was on a roll, but this would prove to be my third and final position at the university. Wait until you hear why.

# Chapter 6:

## My First Vice Presidency at a University: Acting Vice President for Student Affairs

A few years beyond the Ivy League, I found myself where I wanted to be—a Vice President of a state university with managerial, supervisory, and budgetary oversight over staff, departments, and students. I had left academic affairs as Associate Vice President for Administration and had become the new Acting Vice President for Student Affairs. Now I would have academic affairs and student affairs experience on my resume and in my work background. I was elated!

Having lived on at least four college campuses, I can say that the units of the university that I am most familiar with are academic affairs because I was a student who needed to be instructed, and student affairs because I was a student who needed to be housed, given financial aid and other services. Thus from a consumer of services and benefits, academic and student affairs were the most important entities of the university for me. I was about to say the Library was a third important entity for me until I realized that in many universities, the Library is an offshoot of academic affairs or is at least paired closely with that unit.

When you think of student affairs, what do you think of? Is it dormitory or apartment life? Good or bad roommates? Campus life? Concerts and dances? Fraternities and sororities? Football, basketball, and track or swim meets? Homecoming? Parades? Competing for or voting for campus queens, student government association leaders? Financial aid? Cafeteria food? Well, all of these and more come to mind when I think of my time as a student and later my stint as Acting Vice President for Student Affairs. This step in my chosen career path allowed me to manage a student affairs unit that consisted of several departments such as, campus and student life and development, career planning and placement, residence life, university police, student court, and health services. These broad areas included housing, financial aid, job placement, rehabilitation and disability services, testing, counseling, student government, homecoming, sororities and fraternities, other student clubs and organizations, and the cafeteria.

As the chief administrator and supervisor of the managers and staff in these departments, our goal was to enhance the life of students outside of the classroom and contribute to their overall development as they obtained their education and entered into adulthood, a career path, and their future lives.

There were many good activities that happened in the student affairs unit that made the job of Acting Vice President enjoyable. First of all, students were housed in clean, safe dormitories that included good dormitory directors and resident assistants. They had a cafeteria and a snack bar on campus, and a Student Union building with all kinds of activities for students. There were many other activities on campus for them to participate in. Everything from clubs and organizations to Homecoming queen and court, athletic games, intramural games, block dances, parades, and concerts were available.

In addition, students had work-study jobs on campus for pay, job placement with nearby businesses for experience and pay prior to graduation. Counseling services and health services were available and included in their student fees.

Access to staff at the university was readily available. My office and almost all offices on campus including the President's office operated on a walk-in basis for students. They could but did not have to make an appointment to discuss an issue, concern, or problem.

Things started off well and were going along swimmingly for approximately a month or two. After then, I discovered that the work in

My First Vice Presidency at a University:

student affairs was interesting, demanding, stressful, and often political. Some cracks in the surface were beginning to present themselves. When you have the lives of teenagers and young adults in a dormitory environment with all that entails, along with campus life activities, sororities and fraternities, football and basketball games, weekly parties and dances, it is easy to see how the job could be interesting, demanding, and even stressful. That part of the job was doable. The projects, paperwork, and day-to-day management activities were enjoyable, especially since I had competent and conscientious department managers, for the most part.

I must say that I met all deadlines on paperwork and projects that were required of my unit. I even kept each department in line with their budget expenditures. During my tenure as Acting Vice President, I do not recall ever having my paperwork, projects, expenditures, and similar activities called into question. Yet, I failed miserably in one big, main, key area that colored my whole job performance in student affairs. I failed at managing the political problems of my position.

Politics, you may ask, what was so problematic and political about student affairs? Oh really, now. What isn't potentially problematic or political in student affairs? First of all, the student judicial system, student court, for the control of student conduct and misbehavior on campus is very political. Some students would break rules and come to student court prepared with all of their friends as either witnesses or alibis. Mind you, these were usually friends who have a little experience with breaking rules and skirting the system. Many of them have either mastered the art of stretching the truth or telling lies with finesse, or they were in the process of acquiring and refining those skills. Many friends of the student who was summoned to student court showed up as onlookers so they could be tutored in case they ever appeared in court themselves. Who knew if or when they would haze a pledge, break dorm rules, get a traffic ticket on campus, or become creative and inquisitive in their smoking habits?

Without fail in student court, the witnesses proceeded to verify every detail given by their friends who were appearing in court, and of course, the student affairs' employee who was bringing charges was hard pressed to find a witness among students who would testify steadfastly to the misbehavior of another student. Sometimes the only solid witnesses that student affairs had were the university police or the actual employee who charged the student with an infraction. The long and short of it was that the misbehaving student was usually let go with a slap on the wrist or more often no penalty at all.

Another area of student affairs that was problematic and political was fraternity and sorority pledging. It is interesting that fraternities and sororities operate on college and university campuses, yet they are not under the complete control of the college or university that hosts them. Their parent organizations have ultimate control of them and have rules and regulations that govern them. If a fraternity or sorority is found in violation of too many rules, too many times, the university could suspend their operation on campus or, in the case of very serious or very frequent infractions, it could permanently ban them from operating on its campus.

I am not against fraternities and sororities at all. They add a lot of flavor and spice to campus life. Indeed, I pledged a sorority as an undergraduate and enjoyed it immensely. The problem with fraternities and sororities is not the cute color-coded outfits they wear, the nice, rhythmic step shows they perform, or the fun rushes and parties they throw. When there is a problem, it is usually about the forbidden practice of hazing pledges. Some of them still do that even though they know it is wrong and they'll get in trouble if they are caught. There is just something about hazing a person under their supervision who wants to be a part of their organization that is too enticing, intriguing, and alluring to pass up. Some frat brothers or sorority sisters think, why not just beat the pledges? Why not just humiliate them greatly? Why not make them do dangerous things? Why not push them to the point of fear to see how they will think and react under pressure? After all, they want to be a part of our brotherhood or sisterhood and that should be worth something to them. They have to sacrifice their dignity and individuality and show how much they want to be a part of us, don't they? I imagine the above rationale or something similar to it has sparked some wild-sounding prank to turn injurious or in a few cases deadly. I am truly happy that the heavy-duty pledging tactics that inflicted bodily injury, near death, or death never happened on our campus. I have heard of serious hazing incidences on campuses elsewhere, but I am just so, so happy we did not hear of serious, dangerous, heavy-duty hazing happening at our university while I was managing the student affairs unit. You see, out of all of the bad things that did or could have happened, we were spared the worse kind of hazing problems.

Another thing that was problematic and political for me in student affairs was the political clout some elected student leaders carried on the campus. It was not unusual for them to band together against a Student

Affairs Vice President in order to have their way about situations in the unit and about the campus. Many times I felt that they had confused the duties of their elected positions among students with the duties, role, and responsibilities of the Vice President for Student Affairs and staff. These students were not hired, paid, adult employees whose duty it was to supervise and manage the student affairs unit overall. The student governing body was not and should not have been a parallel and opposing organization to the office of student affairs regardless of who was Vice President. But at times it seemed to be at our university. Perhaps this was an anomaly or just my viewpoint or a serious weakness on my part. One reason for this 'parallel and opposing' viewpoint I had was because of the position the chief student leader had on the university's governing board. This seemed to have sandwiched me in, in some cases. In his position as a student, this student leader's position was below mine. In his position as a governing board member, the student held a position that was above mine and even above that of my supervisor, the President.

At any university with such a structure, if and when a student leader and governing board member is opinionated and strong willed and if the Vice President is also opinionated and strong willed, that scenario can create a problem on the day-by-day functioning and management of the student affairs unit. When things don't go the way either of them thinks on an issue, when they don't see eye-to-eye, a political situation brews and sometimes erupts below and above the position of Vice President for Student Affairs. These situations can be testy and difficult to manage if things get out of hand. Additionally, I have always found it difficult to politically manage or refute comments that are made about me, but never to me, especially if those comments are made at very high levels and to very influential people.

Frustration is what results next. One can become frustrated and discouraged because a mound of good work, project completion, and deadlines met can become overshadowed by the inability to manage personalities and politics well. And managing personalities includes one's own personality under pressure as well as others' personalities. Frustration leads to venting at the most inappropriate times and places and in the most awful way even to the persons to whom one should always respect—the university's President. This includes frustration and venting that one regrets even as it is occurring. It is all because of failure and disappointment in one's own eyes, mainly because that is what it appeared to be in others' eyes also. Why am I telling you this? Well, it is because if you have not experienced the kiss or the bite of the political process at work on your job, it is my belief that you will see a little of both before you retire. In fact, I don't know of anyone from the lowest ranking staff person to the highest ranking officer—the President or CEO who has not seen people and situations that either worked in his or her favor or against him or her. If there is such a person out there, I would like to meet him or her. When bad things happen, you might know or want to know that it happens to almost everyone at some point in his or her career. So when ***things*** happen to you, know that you are not alone or unique in this occurrence. Does that make you feel better? It didn't make me feel better when I told this truth to myself over and over again. I felt miserable, ashamed, bested, and defeated. I was happy about my successes and at the same time deflated over my failures or at least my mistakes.

So let's talk about my mistakes, and eventually my exit.

# Chapter 7:
## My Mistakes and My Exit

Everyone makes mistakes, and that is not always a reason to exit an institution or organization. If it were, no one would be left to work anywhere. I made mistakes on my job, but I also had many, many successes on the job that I am so very proud of. I did not leave just because of my mistakes and frustrations. I left because I thought it was time to go and seek other experiences elsewhere rather than stay at the same institution in the same or a different position.

But as I look back, I am not attempting to lead others to believe that they or I have not and will not make mistakes on the job. So, I am willingly recounting and recollecting some of my mistakes as I tell you about my successes.

It was a mistake to not foster better communication between myself as Acting Vice President for Student Affairs and all of the students at the university. Sometimes there is just too much to do and too little time. But if you are a professional in student affairs, try as much as possible to reach and communicate with your students as often as possible. Make them feel cared about and listen to their problems and insecurities and ideas. It can make a difference in their lives on campus and in your life. It might be the case that peer-to-peer communication and relationships among students carry greater weight, and there is nothing wrong with that. After all, it is their college experience. I have had mine and some of you have had yours or will have yours. It was that way when I was an undergraduate student so long ago and it is probably that way now and will be for years to come. I found that no matter how you try to relate and communicate, you are not one of the students on campus and you should not attempt to be one with them.

It was also a mistake for me to believe that others in authority positions who did not supervise my work would perceive me, my work, and efforts the way I saw myself and my contributions. If you have not already done so, you might want to take note of this fact and start trying to do a self-analysis and a little self-promotion of your achievements to the right people at the right time.

It was a mistake to believe that a title, even a high-level one that is one step below President, carried weight and authority and commanded respect due it in and of itself. It was a mistake to believe that hard work in a position is most of what is required of anyone. Hard work is a must, but it is not the standard by which you are always judged. I must say, however, that I have been rewarded almost all of the time for my hard work and diligence and loyalty. But, there comes a time when those characteristics are not enough. It depends on who is viewing you and whether you are well regarded by those who make decisions. You must do the work, but don't neglect the other aspects of the workplace. They, too, are important.

It was a mistake to believe that situations would work themselves out to the right conclusion, the one I desired, with, of course, a little constructive and positive input from me from time to time. It was a mistake to believe that past contributions, no matter how useful they had been, would affect positively the present contributions when things and situations got testy. You, too, will find that different judges come on the scene and so each position and its work must stand on its own merits.

My mistakes led to my most distressing failure of all. My most distressing failure was that I had become a liability to the President and his administration at the university. I was no longer the asset I had prided myself on being. In my most vivid imagination about my future role and contribution at the institution, I had never envisioned or imagined becoming the liability I perceived that I had become. Although I was not a party to conversations, I could sense that pressure was being placed on the President because of tension among students in the student affairs unit and me, the Acting Vice President. These were tensions that I did not deliberately or knowingly cause, but tensions nonetheless that I took some responsibility for, and rightfully so, because I was Acting Vice President for Student Affairs. I think back to my own undergraduate days during the late 1960s when there was student unrest on many college campuses. Those poor Vice Presidents for Student Affairs. We didn't even think of them, their efforts, and their careers. They were not at fault actually. It was a sign of the times. Of course when I was Acting Vice President for Student Affairs in the late 1980s, we had nothing like student unrest. Thank God! We simply had poor communication along with political clout, savvy, and influence in high places or the lack of it. We simply had things said about me in high places to influential people, but they were never said to me nor did these influential people ever give me the courtesy of asking me anything about it. I could only assume that they believed what they had heard.

Things finally came to fruition when I, for the first time, heard directly something a student leader said about me. All of this time, I surmised that these kinds of things were being said about me (though never to me) in board meetings or more accurately in closed committee meetings or informal conversations where I could not hear them. Well, as luck would have it, there I was in an open board meeting when I heard my name being mentioned and a discussion ensued. After the discussion, the board proposed an action with no hint of any kind of input from me or my supervisor being requested. I was happy to hear the conversation and devastated that they saw me sitting there and didn't say anything to me. They just assumed that what they heard was all factual and began to act on it. (Boards can do whatever they please, you know.) I was not asked a single question or given a cursory glance. Now, what would you do? Well, I'll tell you what I did. I approached the microphone and began to speak on my own behalf and to my own point of view and defense. It seemed incredulous that, as a senior-level officer of the university who was present in formal board meetings, that I was not even accorded the courtesy of a comment from me about me. It was assumed that what was said was true, factual, and actionable when, in fact, it was false, incomplete, and opinionated. Now you know I could not let that opportunity pass without intervening, without speaking up for myself—respectfully of course. After I had my say and the meeting was over, the Chairman of the Board came by my office later that day and apologized to me as if he knew he or the board had done something they should not have done.

So that's what I meant when I told you in a previous chapter that little did I know then as Executive Assistant to the President who attended with the President all board meetings and wrote the draft of the minutes, that I would be a hot topic of the board a few years later in a different position—as Acting Vice President for Student Affairs.

Now you might be wondering what I was doing all of this time that strife and tension and politics were occurring and things were being said about me but never to me or in my presence, except at that board meeting I just discussed. Come now. I am not as shy, naive, pathetic, or unschooled as I may seem from what you have just read in this book. Of course I had been planning my exit. But I wanted an exit on my own terms and not on anyone else's terms. I wanted to set things right about me once I heard what was being said and then leave. When the board meeting occurred where I heard for the first time something negative a student leader said about me, a practice that had been going on a long time as rumors have it, I got to defend myself and I received a personal apology from the Board Chairman. That's all I wanted or needed to feel better. You see, I already had in my possession offers for three high-level positions—two offers were from highly-prestigious institutions, and one offer was from a system of seven colleges in the Midwestern United States.

So I wasn't just walking around with my head in the sand doing projects, supervising my student affairs' staff, and meeting deadlines along with all of the other things my position required of me. All along, I was doing what you would have been doing. All along, I was doing what a highly-qualified though unappreciated professional would have been doing. I was looking for another job—planning my exit. There is no such thing as one position and one position only that a professional must have. If I am not appreciated or wanted in one place, I could always take my Harvard doctorate, my experience, and my highly-qualified self elsewhere. And that's what I did. I went happily on my way and thanked God for the experience I had gained during my tenure at the university. I must add that, on the whole, my experiences at the university had been positive ones. The experiences in student affairs had been contrary to the norm.

I will say this to you. Do your job well at all times. I can recall times when I was in my office on campus at 9:30 a.m. on Sunday mornings doing what I needed to do—appreciated or not. Don't expect only positive experiences on a job. Don't believe that everyone else is experiencing rhapsody, pleasure, and complete happiness in the positions they have or have had. The world of work is not like that. It is filled with people, personalities, situations, circumstances, rumors, stresses, and strains. No one is problem free in an environment that contains at least one person other that himself or herself. Different people see the same or different things differently, and they react to these things differently. Students and employees in a college or university are at differing levels of maturity, viewpoints, opinions, responsibilities, and functions. All of their viewpoints are important and they come into play in the environment. It is what makes the workplace challenging, engaging, and instructive. We learn from each other and the environments we create.

Sameness is no fun at all, usually unattainable, and often undesirable if attained. Never stay in one place, position, or organization to the point of becoming bitter and enraged. Find something else more pleasing and suitable to your style and needs. Don't run as soon as you hear one or two negative comments or as soon as you have to fight, win, or lose one or two political battles. You have to mature as an administrator, employee, and a person. You might as well start developing your steadfastness, maturity, experience, and acumen where you are. If you go away immediately, you might only find a 'fresh hell' somewhere else. Then what are you going to do? Are you going to stay packed everywhere you go? Or are you going to employ the 'fight or flight' strategy? You can fight to stay and grow and contribute if it is still worthwhile to you to do so. Or, you can take flight when it is not.

So ultimately what I am saying to you is analyze your situation as honestly and objectively as you can. Do it over and over again to consider as many factors as you can. If it is time to go, go. Just take the time to plan your exit strategy and get another suitable position, if you have time. That's what I did. I enjoyed my stay at the university where I got my first administrative experience, and I will always be grateful to the President and others who hired me, trained me, and allowed me to grow and contribute.

But, the time came for me to leave. I did. But, was it better, worse, or just different?

# Chapter 8:
## The Governing Board

My new position was worse, better, and different—all at the same time. It was worse for camaraderie, better for pay, and different in work assignments. When I left the university where I had held three high-level administrative positions, I accepted a position with the governing board of a system of seven colleges in the Midwest. The system had seven Presidents of the seven colleges and these Presidents reported to a Chancellor who, in turn, reported to the governing board.

My position was unique in higher education in that I, as Director of Board Programs and Policy Analysis, also reported directly to the governing board, but not through the Chancellor. So, there were two employees in the system that reported to the governing board—the Chancellor and I, the Director of Board Programs and Policy Analysis. This arrangement could not be permanent nor did I expect it to be so. But that is what that governing board wanted and you may or may not know that governing boards have a tendency to do as they please regardless of who thinks what or what seems logical or illogical. I am not being hard on or disrespectful of governing boards. I am just stating plainly and bluntly a fact that I observed first hand on more than one occasion with more than one governing board. Indeed, almost all of the administrative positions I have held before and after this one in various higher education institutions either required, allowed, or expected me to be at all regular meetings of the governing board. Only one position, that of Associate Vice President for Academic Affairs, did not require or expect my presence at regular board meetings.

Perhaps the best thing about being Director of Board Programs and Policy Analysis was the opportunity the position gave me to report to the governing board and learn as much as possible about one board before I became a college or university President or Chancellor who was responsible for a host of people below me while being accountable for myself, and for programs, budgets, operations, successes, and failures. A second position reporting to a governing board could not last very long; at least that is what I expected and I was correct. I was in the position a little less than two years. Before the position ended, the board offered me the position of President of one of the seven colleges, which I declined and the Chancellor offered me the position of Vice Chancellor, which I declined. To this day I do not know what I was thinking. I had tried hard, worked hard, and climbed the ladder rung-by-rung to make it to those two positions, and when they were finally offered to me I declined them. Looking back, I wonder why?

During my stay in the system, I observed carefully what I could readily see. In my opinion, the board members were courteous and professional enough, but I thought they placed too much confidence in the integrity, character, and professionalism of the Chairman of the Board. I thought his duplicity and lack of integrity were as obvious to them as they were to me. Perhaps they were and that's why they took a hands-off approach to dealing with him. Judging by some of the things he said to me, all of these characteristics about him were suspect in my opinion. He would always approach me in a very negative fashion and then say if you tell the other board members what I said, I will deny it and then you'll look like a liar. It appears that I was not the only one he used this tactic on.

The board seldom commented on anything the Chairman said in the meetings. I do not recall an outright challenge to his actions, and seldom was a counterproposal put in motion to what the Chairman said or wanted. I am not advocating discord. I only comment because seldom is everything a person says, wants, or does completely representative of everyone's thinking on every subject and every issue. Consequently, discussion often brings to the forefront things that have been overlooked or things that need attention or refocusing. I do recall, on occasions, several board members double-checking on some issues that were proposed or acted on.

Because seldom are anyone's motives completely pure, selfless, and aboveboard, many times I was left wondering about the motives behind comments and exchanges, and often I was struck by the cavalier way major decisions were reached. I am talking about decisions that affected nameless, faceless people's careers and livelihoods. Some people's careers and livelihoods went down the drain with a statement and voice vote or the raising of hands. I certainly do understand that tough decisions have to be made at the appropriate levels, but I was still struck by the ease and sometimes nonchalance in which decisions were made.

Things lumbered along in the system with hiring and firing and programs added, strengthened, or changed. Then it became time for the board to decide on continuing to have two positions report to the board. The entire system reported to the Chancellor and not through me. My position was eliminated. Knowing that I had declined two senior-level administrative positions in the system—college President and Vice Chancellor, I decided not to seek another position in the system. I relocated to a Southern state and city where I had many relatives and where I would be closer to my parents and home state. I had made a full circle or at least a roughly-shaped full circle. I settled in, put down roots, acquainted myself with the city, its attractions, and people along with old friends and began to enjoy my new home immensely. After a while, I began to search for a job. My search landed me two positions in higher education institutions—Academic Advisor at a local prestigious university, and the second position was Vice President for Academic Affairs at a struggling college. I chose the latter position.

Are you beginning to have questions about my decision-making as it concerns my career goals? I am. Read on.

# Chapter 9:

## Vice President for Academic Affairs

In my short time in my new city, I thought back on what I had accomplished and I was pleased, although I still wondered why I had not accepted the college presidency or the vice chancellorship when they were offered. I concluded that my decision had been clouded by emotions, apprehension, and a little of what I had seen from the Chairman of the Board in that short time I had been there. If I were to do it over, I would accept one or both of those positions.

When my position with the governing board ended, I had decided to relocate to an area where I had many relatives, a few high school classmates, and several friends. I had settled in, put down roots, and begun my job search. Finding a suitable job any time one wants to do so is not always easy to do. I had to decide whether I would continue my career in higher education institutions, work with administration in secondary education, or pursue a career outside of the education field. I applied for jobs in those three categories and found the availability of positions limited or uninteresting to me. Before too much time expired, I was offered two positions during the same week—one position was in an academic advising department at a university; the other position was Vice President for Academic Affairs at a local struggling college. I accepted the position with the higher job title, higher responsibilities and reporting level, and most challenges—that of Vice President for Academic Affairs. I was not above being vain and upward looking, even if something in the back of my mind said the position might not be right for me. I soon discovered that the college had financial, physical facility, and academic challenges, in addition to accreditation problems. I was far, far beyond the Ivy League in my career path, wondering about my career decisions, and being certain of only one thing—I had a job. I had gotten to that point in my career.

When I began work at the college, it became obvious to me that it was in flux and in a fix. It needed a lot of care, grooming, and managing in its facilities, programs, policies, and procedures. The financial picture was bleak. The outlook was a bit grim. This was nothing that a bit of hard work could not fix, I thought. So, I immediately rolled up my sleeves and went to work wholeheartedly on properly staffing the academic departments, strengthening the academic programs, meeting or exceeding the accreditation standards in all of our program and curricula areas, and ensuring we met the accreditation requirements for faculty preparation and credentials—all for the good of the college. This was no small task because of time constraints and required no small amount of effort, but I was willing to expend the time and energy because I thought it was worth it for the college and students and community.

The beginning of the school year was rapidly approaching. Faculty needed to be in place in time to do their syllabi and other professional preparation based on the courses they were assigned to teach. Interviewing faculty prospects went at a frantic pace and trying to ensure that we had the right person in the right position in such a short time was mind-boggling and futile. What I had to finally console myself with was that the people I recommended to the President for hire in academic affairs had the proper credentials, the proper years and type of experience, and had done reasonably well in their interviews. Many people could or would meet these criteria. Whether we selected the absolute best person became a relative and moot issue. While the interviewing and hiring processes were a bit difficult and uncertain, the pool of candidates from which we chose was the easy part. We had no shortage of applicants for each position. The files were bursting at the seams, and additional boxes and boxes of resumes were stacked near the files. It seemed as if most people were looking for a job or, at least, a change from their current positions and situations. One thing that complicated the process was the fact that the college was nearing an accreditation visit. As Vice President for Academic Affairs, I had to be extra vigilant and careful to review the existing faculty and their credentials before and while hurriedly recommending new faculty to fill vacant positions. You see, each person I recommended had to have a master's or doctor's degree in his or her teaching specialty, and his or her credentials had to help us meet accreditation standards in the department and major area in which he or she was recommended. I did not have the luxury of recommending for hire someone who had excellent credentials and would have made a superb addition to the academic community at the college. I had to forego these types of recommendations in favor of even a less-spectacular applicant who had the necessary credentials to meet accreditation criteria in an area where the college had a weakness. To be sure, budget constraints were huge dictating factors of any action I took. Those of you who are or who have been in a position to hire or recommend for hire know what I mean and how it feels to overlook a stellar resume and an extremely well- qualified, interested, and interesting applicant in favor of putting those dollars to use in areas that must be shored up to preserve the college and/or a program.

After the faculty had been hired, the problems, opportunities, and challenges did not end. They escalated. Office space had to be completed and assigned. You might ask, why all of these kinds of problems? Well, perhaps I did not mention that the college itself was in the process of moving into a different facility. That is why the need to hire a larger faculty and reestablish basic services existed. Books were scarce or nonexistent, and distributing supplies to teachers was unheard of at this poor, financially-strapped college. To add to the problems, science laboratories were inadequate, not set up, and needed renovating and improving. The library needed books, books, and more books. Added to this, the resource room for faculty to copy materials and do their work in was not in operation. The academic unit was on its own and in a fix. It was a kind of fix that I had no experience with; I had never worked in a situation where resources of all kinds were in such short supply, and with no solution in sight. So, we had to adapt to the situation, provide our own supplies and resources, and still get the job done and done well. The good part about it was that these things were only inconveniences. They did not affect master's degree and doctor's degree faculty's knowledge of subject matter and their ability to enter a classroom and teach their students the subject matter that they were so adequately prepared to teach. All of the things I've mentioned are commonplace in and descriptive of poorly-funded, no-frills colleges and universities in the United States and in some other countries around the world.

Those who choose to be a part of these arenas, as I had chosen to be, know that they must contribute or supply resources of their own when and where possible. They must share cramped, inadequate, and non-posh office spaces, overlook inconveniences, be patient with slow to no progress, and look within themselves for job satisfaction. But teach and teach well they must do. Those who are administrators must do their jobs, too, within the same limiting and constraining environment. To be honest, sometimes it became tiring, stressful, and even unbearable day after day with the same budget constraints and the accompanying problems. But we continued on. Others and I tried to think of the job before us, of what needed to be done, and especially of what had to be done. And what had to be done in my administrative area was to prepare for the upcoming accreditation visit. So, that's what I did. That's what I put my mind, my talent, my energy toward getting done.

A visit from the regional accreditation body is probably the most serious of all visits and outward influences on a college or university. Colleges and universities must be accredited for their work and their degrees to mean anything. Colleges and universities must be accredited in order to remain in operation. My duty as Vice President for Academic

## Vice President for Academic Affairs

Affairs was to play a huge and paramount role in the process of gaining and keeping the college accredited by the regional accreditation agency. This required a huge amount of work and attention to details in every aspect and program of the college.

We undertook a thorough assessment and evaluation of each program in the academic affairs' area at the college, and I was especially careful to ensure that we met or exceeded the percent of doctorate or terminal degrees required to teach in each academic degree program. I personally made sure of that. We could not take a chance on this requirement not being met because it would put the college in dire straits and in danger of losing its accreditation After the visit, the President was informed that the college had retained its accreditation, but had a few requirements that must be met. Needless to say, everyone was excited and elated with the news. With this hurdle cleared, we could all breathe a sigh of relief and settle into our routine duties of teaching or managing a program, department, or unit of the college.

Then something terrible happened to me. At least I thought it was terrible at the time, but time proved me wrong. Problems, internal conflicts, personality clashes, and egos were rampant and did not diminish. They escalated and became a day to day distraction in the world of work among quite a few people and resulted in the President, others, and me being let go, *fired*, while a few who should have been let go or fired were retained. At the time, this was a terrible blow to me, but the impact did not last long. The realization that I was fired from a struggling college that I had worked so hard to position properly academically smacked of unfairness, ingratitude, and lack of respect. I was fired. Who would have thought it? And it was done in such a cowardly way—a letter with no signature in an envelope slid under my door. Yes, as qualified as I, Dr. Chase, was with my resume showing years of experience. I, with my Harvard doctorate, hard work, successful results, was not wanted. The college had been on probation from the regional accreditation body when I got there, something I was not told until after I was hired, and something that required me to work strenuously day and night to correct and prevent my name and reputation from being sullied with a college that met its demise while I was the newly-hired Vice President for Academic Affairs.

Rage hit me for a moment, but only for a moment. Then relief and a calm peacefulness came over me. I could and would do better than this. Certainly I could and would go elsewhere where there were adequate finances, facilities, and all types of resources to fit the employees, students, and programs of the institution, but I would remain in the city and state that I had grown to love and call home. I would accept whatever position that became available to me and not search for the highest-level positions that would require me to relocate. Yes, I would go somewhere where there was more professionalism, much more professionalism. These thoughts came to my mind for about ten minutes after I read that cowardly, unsigned letter that was slid under my door. I told the lady in human resources about the letter that she knew nothing about, and within twelve minutes after picking the letter up from the floor, I walked to my car and drove away from the campus with a freed spirit that had just a little spark of anger around the edges.

My only unfinished business was getting my contract paid. That was done with just one visit from my attorney to the interim "President" the board had hired. Once my pay was obtained, I was satisfied and free to go elsewhere where I belonged. But the nerve of them to wait until I removed the academic programs of the college from accreditation probation and then fire me and others who had managed the larger units and done the bulk of the important work at the college. Some would say that an ***unsigned*** letter under your door is not a true firing, but who cares about technicalities. The main point is that if the college did not want me, I certainly did not want them or need whomever it was that sent me that letter.

Yes, as qualified as you may be fellow Ivy-League graduate and non-Ivy-League graduate alike, you, too, can and probably will be downsized, let go, or fired (What I call it) at least once in your career. If not, then you are a better man or woman than I. Why am I telling you all of this? Well, if you have not had much experience in the work world, I want you to be aware of the kinds of things that can or will happen, especially at high levels in an institution or organization. I also want you to know that ***you do not always have to be at fault to be let go or fired.*** I was never told a reason for my firing nor did the person give me the courtesy of a face-to-face meeting looking me in the eyes. I did not even rate a signed letter. I am not bitter, just expressive. With a little nudging, I got myself out of the wrong arena and put myself into an arena that was more of a proper fit for me, my qualifications, experience, work ethic, efforts, and liking.

Another reason why I am telling you this is because no matter how hard you or others work, how valuable your contributions are, or whether they are recognized, acknowledged, or even appreciated, you can be downsized, let go, or fired. It is not a new phenomenon. Others do not always see or value you as you see or value yourself. In many States, there is no guaranteed right to work. It might not feel good even if you know it is for the better in the long run, even if you know that you will be all right or even much better off. You can, should, and must move on to bluer skiers, greener pastures, and better opportunities and positions. They are out there. Things can and will get better. That is what happened to and for me. I did something that I had always wanted to do as a professional. My new job was a more peaceful and professional environment that I welcomed, and I realized how much I had been missing those aspects of the work environment in my life.

# Chapter 10:
## Consulting and College Teaching

I started working for myself, consulting professionally, and setting my own workload. I did consulting work from my home office. I will tell you about one of my consulting projects that I especially liked.

I worked through a professional company of psychologists, social workers, and attorneys who did consulting for large, established law firms. Part of my doctorate is in social policy in education, but I worked in that area as a jury consultant helping to educate and prepare potential participants in legal cases on the social aspects of the legal process. Of course, in a trial, the judge is legally prepared as are the attorneys, but the jury is not. Juries operate more often in the area of social policy. What seems right in the eyes and minds of reasonable, lay citizens who hear evidence being presented is what makes a jury work. They are not trained in the law.

As a consultant at the company, I worked primarily with the initial interviewing of witnesses, with witness school, with mock trials, with the debriefing of the mock jury, and with post-trial interviews of actual jurors in the actual case presented in court and decided by a jury. When I first started my work in social policy, I was fascinated with witness school. A big part of witness school was keen observation of actual witnesses as they took the witness stand in the company's courtroom and began testifying. We the staff of attorneys, psychologists, social workers, social policy analysts, trial scientists, and others observed and scrutinized the witness closely for appearance, body language, appropriate dress, posture, eye contact, believability, nervousness, and other facets of social interaction. We rated the witness on a common scale and offered constructive comments on what the witness did, how he or she could improve the social aspects of testifying, how an actual jury might view the witness, and how the witness might improve on those factors. However, we, the company's staff did not critique, comment on, intervene in or influence the actual facts of the witnesses' testimony. That was strictly the purview of the witness and his or her attorneys.

There have been many instances when we discussed dress, eye contact, and body language that some witnesses did not seem very cognizant of the fact that these factors play as much a role in the eyes of the jury when they make a decision as do the testimony the witnesses give and the evidence the attorneys present. In the absence of legal training, the jurors rely on what they have readily available—reasonable viewpoints influenced by facts, testimony, and evidence presented to them, and a common-sense approach to what they can see, deduce, and believe for themselves. As a testament to juries, I think the system works more often than it does not. Jurors are presented mountains of conflicting testimony from witnesses, experts in the field, and sometimes the defendants themselves. Along with this come exhibit after exhibit of facts and materials put in evidence. Sometimes there are cases on financial matters from brokers, analysts, planners, and corporations that must be decided by jurors who do not have special expertise in these areas of specialization or in these areas of the law. I often wonder why jurors do not yarn, yawn, sleep, or at least tune out these kinds of cases that drag on and on. On the whole, jurors do a remarkable job of sorting through fact and fiction, truth and lies to reach as fair and equitable a decision as they can. All the while, they are functioning in the arena of what I call social policy. Once seated, many jurors take their roles seriously and try to do a credible job for the system. I, too, took my job seriously and I liked dealing in this area on the fringes of the legal process without my being an attorney.

So, what was a typical day like for me as a social policy analyst/jury consultant? Well, for witness school, I usually conducted an interview of a prospective witness who needed the company's help. Then we placed the witness on the witness stand under examination while the staff assembled in the jury box, rated, and critiqued the witness. After this, we completed our individual evaluations and submitted them to be compiled into one report for the client law firm of the company. Often a prospective witness in a case required a follow-up visit or two before going into court for the actual case.

For mock trials, we assembled mock juries similar to the process the county or district courts used. The mock jurors assembled in the jury box in the private courtroom and listened to a mini-case being presented by the actual attorneys in the case. Then they would break for lunch and reassemble in the jury room to discuss and decide the case. After the discussion and decision, another staff member or I usually debriefed the mock jury as the client attorneys monitored the entire process in a separate room. Staff evaluations and jury debriefing results were compiled for a report or work product to be presented to the client law firm. I am certain that they found tons of information and help for the actual trial in a state or federal courthouse.

Sometimes I performed post-trial interviews of actual jurors in real courtroom cases. It was often very important and informative to attorneys to hear from actual jurors in a case after it had been decided. Additionally, interviewing actual jurors by phone after a trial was one of my favorite projects.

While the work was interesting, rewarding, organized, and professionally done, I eventually stopped consulting with the company because the out-of-town travel required was very stressful and taxing on me, making it difficult for me to continue a large part of the job. Consequently, I sought employment that did not require me to travel out of town at all. I had been a college and university administrator, a consultant, and now I was about to embark upon another facet of a professional educator's career. I was about to become a full-time college/university professor.

I secured a job teaching mathematics fulltime at a local university. This required either a master's or doctor's degree with at least 18 graduate credit hours in mathematics. Luckily, I have two master's degrees. The first one is in Mathematics Education, and the second one is in Education. I had used the second master's and my doctorate in Administration, Planning, and Social Policy in my positions as a college/university administrator and as a social policy analyst/jury consultant. Now, I decided to use the first master's degree in Mathematics Education and become a fulltime mathematics professor. I had never taught fulltime at the college level before. I was a fulltime high school mathematics teacher and a part-time mathematics professor at a university prior to entering Harvard. So, this was another new and fascinating venture for me as I became Professor Chase.

I anxiously arrived early, wide-eyed, and with a smile for my interview and later for my first day of professorial employment in my new job. I went through the usual process in human resources and, afterward, was handed over to my immediate supervisor who assigned me office space, a file cabinet, textbooks, other materials, and sample syllabi. Next she showed me resource rooms for faculty that contained copiers, reams and reams of paper, and all kinds of supplies that would prove useful to any professor. Introductions to department members and other administrative staff and university faculty followed. At the end of the day, I was happy, tired, and at home at my new university. At the time, I did not know that this would be my last job before I retired, but I liked this position, the staff, my supervisor, the students, the entire university, and it appeared that they all liked me back. So I stayed and stayed until I retired because of my disability. I wasn't ready to leave. I became disabled and I had to retire because of that.

However, while I was there, I found the kind of joy and contentment that an educator should have. The joy of imparting knowledge and interacting daily with student learners who were both traditional and nontraditional in ages, learning styles, goals, objectives, career outlook, focus, and abilities. Variety was the name of the game. It never grew boring in the classroom. How could it when the realities of teaching unfolded? There were concepts to teach, reteach, explain, and re-explain. I made lots of assignments. Some students turned them in; others did partial or no homework and assignments. Excuses were tossed about frequently and test days brought on the jitters to nervous students who had procrastinated, to serious students who were poor test takers, and to hardworking, excellent students who were dissatisfied with anything less than an 'A' or 'B.' Yes, this was educators' heaven. Unlike high school, there were extremely few to no disciplinary problems. We were dealing with high school graduates who had chosen to continue their education, along with adults who had chosen to begin college or return to college. Like high school, I had to do some handholding. After all, I was teaching mathematics, which is not a favorite subject for many people. Additionally, some students who were recent high school graduates had been low performers in algebra or had not taken much algebra at all. Many of the mid-twenties to forty-year-old students who were returning to school from the work world had the proper amounts of motivation, but they, too, suffered from weak math skills from high school or perhaps if they had once been good math students, time and distance from those years had made their skills a little 'rusty.' They, too, benefitted from a little handholding. I was happy to oblige. I, too, was subject to regress on skills that I seldom used over the years.

One thing I liked about the life of a professor was the focus on students and classes. The classes I taught were Basic Algebra and College Algebra in that I taught students who were in the first year or year and a half of their academic degree programs. I spent a lot of time explaining in step-by-step details the different types of problems in a skills set. I was often careful to state the rule or rules for each step of problem solving. This helped students understand the reasoning behind the algorithmic process. I would vary this by writing a step and asking them for the property or rule that allowed it. That started and kept them studying the properties in algebra. Even now, I can almost hear the sound of the pages flipping back and forth as my students sought the name and substance of algebraic properties.

One of the things I enjoyed and appreciated most was the willingness to try hard and persistently to succeed and pass the class that my older students demonstrated. It is amazing how many times they would remain after class and approach my desk with a smile if they received a graded paper with a good grade on it. By the same token, you may be able to imagine seeing a grown woman or man cry or fight back tears in their eyes if they had the misfortune of getting a poor grade on a returned paper. These students made sure they waited until everyone left and only they and I were in the classroom. "Here goes," I would say to myself. I knew what they wanted to talk about and what response they wanted from me. Finally, the disappointed student(s) would say, "I thought sure I did better than this" or "I studied so hard" or

"I thought I understood" or "It looks so easy when you explain it on the board." I would always acknowledge their pain courteously and kindly. I am not in the business of hurting students or being cruel or earning a reputation as the "hard, tough one." I'd much rather be known as the helpful one, the encouraging one, the one who explains well and makes it look so easy, the thorough one, the one who is always on task and wastes no time in class. Most of the time, I was all of these. I prided myself on having and maintaining a good, mutually respectful relationship with my students.

As I said, poor performing older students with their 'rusty' skills always came around the desk teary-eyed and nervous after a poor performance. They would say something like, "Can I have extra-credit work to pull up this score?"

I usually said, "If you can't do these problems for regular credit, how are you going to do them for extra credit?"

To this response, they would just hump their shoulders or look down at the floor. I knew what they wanted. They wanted something totally different from these problem sets. Having given them this reality check and further assuring them and me that they could not get something for little or nothing just because they did poorly, I usually made them an extra-credit assignment that they could do for five or ten points. They readily jumped at these assignments and I must say they did quite a bit of work on them. What kinds of extra-credit assignments did I usually make? One assignment was doing reports on mathematicians who had done considerable work in a certain area that we were studying or had studied. For example, when we studied the Cartesian coordinate system or graphing in a plane, I would assign them a project or report on French mathematician Rene Descartes. Students would use the internet to synthesize information and write their reports to turn in for extra credit, and either the first ten minutes or last ten minutes of class those who had researched and written the mathematician reports would present them to the entire class. Another extra-credit assignment was the math puzzles of skill sets we had covered and in which they needed reviews of past materials covered.

It is valuable and admirable for any student to want to continue his or her education beyond high school. This is especially true of thirty- or forty-year-old students who return to college after having been in the work world for a while and having seen for themselves the value of further education. Returning to school usually results from being passed over several times for promotions. It is disheartening for anyone to work faithfully on a job and find that factors other than work ethic are holding them back. These factors can be a combination of office politics, supervisor's assessments and evaluations, personality or lack of it, internal conflicts, budgetary constraints, or insufficient education and credentials to meet requirements for attaining the next rung on the ladder of success. When these students returned to school/college because of insufficient educational backgrounds, my role as a freshman instructor was to aid them as much as possible in their quest for further education or degree completion.

## Consulting and College Teaching

Some students who returned to college did so because they had grown tired of constantly training employees who eventually became their bosses. All companies hire new employees who have degrees and work experience, but who need to be trained for specifics of the new company. Too, all companies hire new college graduates who do not have work experience at other companies or at that company. These two groups of employees are placed in departments and are left to be trained by the existing employees of that department to some extent. Once they are trained by the rank-and-file employees, they become supervisors and proceed to advance further and faster up the ladder of success, leaving behind those with years of experience but marginal credentials. These marginally-credentialed employees do the bulk of the day-to-day work and the training of yet another group of newly-hired degreed employees each quarter or year. Some of my students would speak about this with a look of horror or disgust on their faces. "I can't take any more of that. Something has to change," is usually how they ended the conversation.

Students sometimes cited a third reason for returning to college. Namely, they needed a skills boost because of the rapid changes that advanced technology had brought about. Nothing remains the same. The skills set they entered the job market with was rapidly becoming obsolete. The skills set you begin a career with is not the set of skills with which you will end your career. Growth occurs somewhere between the beginning and the end. Employees gain skills, improve skills, or discard obsolete ones in the process of getting and remaining current, being productive, and managing a career.

Yes, with the combination of traditional-aged students and the non-traditional-aged students, I found quite a bit of pleasure and satisfaction as a university professor. I settled down for the long run and taught to my heart's content.

Then when I found that my disability caused me to be physically unable to do the job, I reluctantly retired. I had come to the end of a good career in higher education. You may know from reading this book that I seemed to have done it in reverse order. I started near the top administratively. I ended it in the classroom as a tenured professor. That worked so well for me. I would not have wanted to do it in customary order—too traditional and conventional for me.

Now I had to decide what, if anything, I could or would do in retirement. Then suddenly I had an idea. See for yourself what it was, next.

# CHAPTER 11:
## Retirement and Writing

My career as a college/university Professor continued along a productive and satisfying path until it came time for me to leave that world behind. I retired and was given a retirement lunch with colleagues and a beautiful engraved plaque commemorating my service at the university. I treasure them both along with my time with my students. But, all things must eventually end. It had been thirty-four years since I first graduated college, and I looked back then and now on a successful life, a successful career, and a successful exit from the world of work.

I started my professional career as a high school teacher; then, I became a graduate teaching assistant at a large state university before going to Harvard. After graduate school and the doctoral degree, I began my career as a university administrator. I was Executive Assistant to the President, Associate Vice President for Academic Affairs, and Acting Vice President for Student Affairs at one university where I contributed and contributed and learned and learned from the President how to become an effective administrator, how to work hard, and how to become successful in my career—a career that I owe, in part, to his help and example. Then, I became Director of Governing Board Programs and Policy Analysis, Vice President for Academic Affairs, Consultant, and University Professor. This was a summary of my life *Beyond The Ivy League.* I chose a career path and I was satisfied with my choices through great times and unsettling times, and through ups and downs. I discovered, as you have or will, that there is no path that is completely straight nor is there one that is devoid of potholes and pitfalls. My career is what I made of it. Yours, too, has been or will be what you make of it. Enjoy the ride. Contribute as much as possible; then contribute some more. Serve the students or, depending on your work, customers, or clients well. Never let it be said that you did not do your job well and to the best of your ability. When you leave your career, celebrate life, what was, and what new things will be. Embark upon your retirement and future goals with gusto and much anticipation.

I chose for my retirement activities rest, relaxation, Bible-study classes, and writing books. I have always wanted to study the Bible systematically the way I studied biology or history, but without the grade. I finally found that opportunity with an organization that is in many parts of the world and that conducts Bible-study in an organized, small group, lecture, written lessons format. I am learning a lot and loving it. I am equally as excited about writing books during my retirement.

My first book was published and it earned four stars out of five from a professional book-reviewing organization. My first book is entitled, **FROM THE FARM TO HARVARD: *My Amazing Journey***. This book, **BEYOND THE IVY LEAGUE: *A Chosen Career Path***, is the sequel and second book. Both are autobiographical in nature and personal memoirs. In both of them, I remember that I have had the time of my life. Looking back, I would choose the same educational and career paths with maybe a few deviations here and there. If I had to do it over, I would accept two positions that were offered to me, but I declined them. I should have accepted the college presidency when it was offered to me. I should have accepted the position of Vice Chancellor in a system of seven colleges, but I declined this position as well. I made a mistake declining both of these offers. What was I thinking then? I don't even remember at this time. But what I do remember is that, on the whole, my educational and career pursuits served me well, and I have told you the good and not so good points, the successes and stresses of my jobs. I absolutely love the personal and professional success they have afforded me, and, as I continue to write, I hope that you will find something about my story and journey as recorded in these two books admirable, amusing, interesting, inspiring, motivating, and rewarding.

After all, I have gone *FROM THE FARM TO HARVARD* and *BEYOND THE IVY LEAGUE*.

**Pearl Chase**

# APPENDIX
## THE IVY LEAGUE COLLEGES AND UNIVERSITIES

(**NOTE**: All of the information in this Appendix came from sources other than the Author, Pearl Chase. The primary sources are the websites of the eight Ivy League Colleges and Universities. They are listed in the Resources section of this book.)

The Ivy League is an awesome and wonderful set of eight institutions in the Northeastern or New England section of the United States. These eight institutions of higher learning are unsurpassed in people's perception and their role in higher education in America and in many places in the world. In actuality, the title "Ivy League" was originally used to refer to the athletic conference to which these colleges and universities belong. But now the title "Ivy League" is used to represent academic excellence and the following institutions: Brown University in Providence, Rhode Island; Columbia University in New York, New York; Cornell University in Ithaca, New York; Dartmouth College in Hanover, New Hampshire; Harvard University in Cambridge, Massachusetts; Princeton University in Princeton, New Jersey; The University of Pennsylvania in Philadelphia, Pennsylvania; and Yale University in New Haven, Connecticut. These colleges and universities are among the oldest institutions of higher education in the United States. Nine colleges were chartered before the American Revolution. Seven of the nine are in the Ivy League. Two universities were chartered before the American Revolution and are not Ivy League. They are The College of William and Mary in Virginia, which was founded and chartered in 1693, and Queen's College or Rutgers, the State University of New Jersey which was founded and chartered in 1766. Cornell University, founded in 1865, is the only member of the Ivy League universities that was founded after the American Revolution of 1776.

To tell you a little bit about the Ivy League schools, I went to the history and fact sheet of each university's web site and to other sources to glean and summarize information and present it to you. I will describe the universities in the order in which they were founded and chartered. As you might expect, Harvard University is first. Here goes.

Harvard University in Cambridge, Massachusetts: Harvard was founded as "New College" in 1636 in what is now Cambridge, Massachusetts. The name was changed from "New College" to Harvard College after a young minister named John Harvard left his library and half his estate to the college. The institution's endowment has grown steadily over the years, to say the least. It now has an endowment of approximately $32 billion as of 2012, which is the largest university endowment in the world. Harvard has approximately 17 million volumes in its more than seventy libraries, making it the largest university library in the world. As of the 2010-2011 academic year, the university had about 2100 faculty members and 21,000 students. About 6700 of the 21,000 students are undergraduates in Harvard College and about 14,500 students are in the Graduate and Professional Schools.

The student body make-up in Fall 2010 was almost evenly split between male and female students. It is about 50%–50% among undergraduates in the College, and 48% female and 52% male in the Graduate and Professional Schools and the Extension School. By ethnicity, the breakout is as follows: Asian/Pacific Islander 12.5%, Black 5.6%, Hispanic 5.8%, International students 20%, Native American .4%, Multi-race 2.0%, White 43.8%, Unknown 9.8%.

Harvard University is comprised of the undergraduate Harvard College, ten Graduate Schools, and the Radcliffe Institute of Advanced Study. The ten graduate schools and the Radcliffe Institute of Advanced Study were established in this order: the medical school in 1782, the divinity school in 1816, the law school in 1817. It is the oldest continuously operating school of law in the United States. In 1847, Harvard established the Lawrence Scientific School, which became the school of engineering in 2007. The dental school was established in 1867, and the graduate school of arts and sciences was established in 1872. In 1908, the Harvard Business School was established. The Harvard Graduate School of Education (HGSE) became a part of the university in 1920. It is this School that I attended in the mid to late 1980s. After the graduate school of education was established in 1920, the school of public health was founded two years later in 1922. In 1936, two graduate schools were established at Harvard. One was the graduate school of design, and the other was the graduate school of public administration which was renamed the Kennedy School of Government thirty years later in 1966. Currently it has the name Harvard Kennedy School of Government. Radcliffe College, which was chartered in 1894, ceased to operate as an undergraduate college for women at Harvard, and in 1999 it became the Radcliffe Institute for Advanced Study.

Every college or university needs a good leader. Harvard is currently being led by its 28th President, Drew Gilpin Faust, the first female to hold the esteemed office of President of Harvard University. Dr. Faust became President in 2007 after having held positions of Dean of Radcliffe Institute of Advanced Study, the Annenburg Professor of History at the University of Pennsylvania. President Faust received her bachelor's degree in History from Bryn Mawr College, and her master's and doctor's degrees in American Civilization from the University of Pennsylvania. In addition to Dr. Drew Faust, Harvard has had many notable and esteemed Presidents in its history including ministers who were the first Presidents of the College. Here are a few notable Presidents.

Henry Dunster, 1640-1654. Dunster received his B.A. and M.A. degrees from Cambridge University in England. During Dunster's administration, the governing board called the President and Fellows of Harvard College, was established and the young College was chartered in 1650. This made it the oldest corporation in the United States and in the Western Hemisphere. "VERITAS" a Latin word for "truth" was also proposed as Harvard's motto.

Charles Chauncy, 1654-1672, became President after Henry Dunster and under his administration, the country's first university press started operating in Harvard Yard. In 1663, it published the 1200 page Indian Bible which is the first Bible printed in the United States. Also under Chauncy, Caleb Cheeshahleaumawk became the first Indian to earn a Harvard degree in 1665.

Increase Mather was President of Harvard College from 1685 to 1701, leading up to the founding of Yale College in Connecticut.

John Leverett, 1708-1724, was Harvard's first non-clergy President. The oldest structure in the present-day Harvard Yard, Massachusetts Hall, was built in 1720 during Leverett's time in office. Massachusetts Hall houses the Office of the President of Harvard University. Also, the oldest endowed chair at Harvard, the Hollis Professorship of Divinity, was established in 1721 during Leverett's administration and the first student publication, the Telltale, was begun. Leverett's administration saw the organization of the first student club at the College in 1719.

John Quincy, 1829-1845, was a graduate of Harvard College. During his administration, the Harvard Bicentennial of 1836 took place, and the motto "VERITAS" that had been first proposed in 1643 was displayed prominently. It has been used as a motto since that that time. The School's Alma Mater, "Fair Harvard," was also sung first during Quincy's administration. It, too, has been sung ever since.

Thomas Hill, 1862-1868, was the first Harvard President who had been a college President before. He was the former President of Antioch College.

Charles William Eliot, who graduated the college as a chemist, was the longest serving Harvard President. Among his achievements are the introduction of letter grades, the student elective system of courses, the erection of most of the famous "gates" and fences around Harvard Yard, the chartering of Radcliffe College (Harvard education for women) in 1894, and the first Harvard-Yale football game in 1875. Eliot retired as the university's first President Emeritus.

A(bbott) Lawrence Lowell, 1909-1933, developed the house system of dormitory, academic, and student life in 1930-1931 for upper class students. Freshmen students were housed in dormitories on Harvard Yard. Lowell expanded the physical plant and completed many of the classroom buildings outside of Harvard Yard for the graduate schools. He saw the establishment of the school of education in 1920 and the school of public health in 1922. Academically, Lowell introduced general examinations, majors, and tutorials.

James Bryant Conant, 1933-1953, was president during Harvard's 300th birthday in 1936. It was the Tercentenary Celebration. Conant implemented university professors for cross-disciplinary research and national scholarships for exceptionally talented students who were not financially well off, plus he headed the commission that formed the Educational Testing Service (ETS) in 1947. He allowed Radcliffe women to begin attending classes with the men enrolled in Harvard College in the 1940s.

Derek Curtis Bok, 1971-1991, 2006-2007, earned his B.A. degree from Stanford and J.D. degree from Harvard Law School. He later served as dean of Harvard Law before becoming President twice. Bok introduced the core curriculum for undergraduates and oversaw the equal access and gender-blind admission and financial aid policies.

Dr. Bok was President of Harvard during my stay for master's and doctor's degrees in the 1980s.

The university is not devoid of a bit of colorful history. For example, one of Harvard's Presidents, Samuel Locke, 1770-1773, resigned because he reportedly fathered a child by his maid. Another President, Joseph Willard, 1781-1804, had been a butler at the College. A famous murder took place at the Medical School during President Jared Sparks' administration when in 1849 John Webster killed George Parkman (both faculty members) over a loan. Webster was found guilty and hanged a year later. Yet another President, Thomas Hill, is said to have shocked the people of Cambridge, Massachusetts when he parted with the dignity of a Harvard President by stripping off his coat to plant ivy beside the library!! Such actions did not seem to match the picture people had in mind of a Harvard President.

A university is nothing without its students and what they do during and after their matriculation at the campus. Former Harvard students continue to perform well and rise to elevated positions in the United States and worldwide. Out of forty-four U.S. Presidents, eight or 18% of them have been Harvard graduates. They are John Adams, John Quincy Adams, Rutherford B. Hayes, Theodore Roosevelt, Franklin Delano Roosevelt, John Fitzgerald Kennedy, George Walker Bush, and Barack Hussein Obama, who in 2008 became the current U. S. President and the first African American President of the United States of America.

The University has had 50 Nobel Prize laureates, 35 Pulitzer Prize winners, and many MacArthur Fellows or "genius" award winners..

The Harvard website cites *Business Insider* as listing thirty of the most famous Harvard students of all times. The list is impressive. It includes in no special order Stanley Marcus of Neiman Marcus stores, Sumner Redstone, CEO of National Amusements, Incorporated, whose family is majority owner of CBS Corporation, Viacom, MTV Networks, BET, Paramount Pictures, and DreamWorks. Other CEOs included are James McNerney, CEO of Boeing, Lloyd Blankfein, CEO and Chairman of Goldman Sachs Group, Incorporated, Bill Gates, Co-Founder, Chairman, President, CEO of Microsoft Corporation, and Mark Zuckerberg, Founder of Facebook. Other famous Harvard students have served in government and public service other than the eight U.S. Presidents. Some of them are Al Gore, former Vice President of the United

States during the President Bill Clinton administration and former candidate for President of the United States. Also included are Mitt Romney, former Governor of Massachusetts and candidate for the Republican Party nominee for President of the United States. John Roberts, Chief Justice of the United States Supreme Court, David Souter, Justice of the U.S. Supreme Court, Ben Bernanke, Chairman of the U.S. Federal Reserve, Lawrence Summers, former U.S. Treasury Secretary and former President of Harvard University, Mike Crapo, U.S. Senator from Idaho, Jennifer Granholm, Governor of Michigan, and Felipe Calderon, President of Mexico.

In the entertainment and communications industry, the list includes Jack Lemmon, John Lithgow, Tommy Lee Jones, Bill O'Reilly, Jr., Ashley Judd, Matt Damon, and Natalie Portman. The list is not exhaustive. There are many, many notable former Harvard students and graduates in the U.S. and worldwide who have excelled in their endeavors.

With all of the facts and figures out of the way, let's take a brief look at the campus itself and some of the social activities of its students. The most notable and well-known part of Harvard University is Harvard Yard, the area that represents the original part of Harvard that dates back to 1636. The Yard is approximately twenty-five acres of dormitories, office buildings, and the main library, Widener Library. They surround an open courtyard known as Tercentenary Theatre. It is Tercentenary Theatre that hosts commencement, centennials, and other university-wide ceremonies. Widener Library on Harvard Yard along with the university's 70+ other libraries is the world's largest university library. Currently it has more than seventeen million volumes.

There are many student activities at the campus. Among them are Phi Beta Kappa, the student newspaper, the band, rowing and other athletic teams, and the famed competition—the Harvard-Yale football game which began in 1875.

(www.harvard.edu/president/biography, 11/18/11). www.harvard.edu/history/presidents, 11/18/11.

THE IVY LEAGUE COLLEGES AND UNIVERSITIES

WHEW! That brings us to a short historical look at our second Ivy-League University—Yale University. Note that one College, William and Mary in Virginia, was founded in 1693 prior to Yale's founding. It is the second of the colleges founded in the colonies, but it is not a part of the Ivy League. Thus, Yale is the third college founded in the colonies, but it is the second of those that are in the Ivy League.

Yale University in New Haven, Connecticut: Yale was founded in 1701 in Saybrook, Connecticut "to educate students for Publick employment both in Church & Civil State." It moved to New Haven in 1716. The College was named in 1718 for a Welsh merchant named Elihu Yale who gave the College money, more than 400 books, and a portrait of King George I. Yale established graduate schools in the early 1800s with the Yale school of medicine established in 1810, divinity in 1822, law in 1824, graduate school of arts and sciences in 1847, art in 1869, music in 1894, forestry and environmental studies in 1900, nursing in 1923, drama in

1955, architecture in 1972, and management in 1974. Yale awarded the first Ph.D. in the United States in 1861. The university began admitting women at the graduate level in 1869 and at the undergraduate level in 1969. In 1876, Yale awarded the first Ph.D. to an African American in the United States. His name was Edward A. Bouchet and he was an 1874 graduate of Yale College. His doctorate was in Physics and it was the sixth doctorate in Physics ever awarded. Currently, Yale's libraries hold 12.7 million volumes. Its endowment is 16.1 billion, and the university has 3695 faculty as of 2009-2010.

As of Fall 2010, Yale had approximately 11,000 students from the United States and worldwide in its undergraduate, graduate, and professional schools programs. The enrollment is almost 50%–50% between male and female students. By ethnicity, the breakout is as follows: American Indian/Alaska Native less than 1%, Asian 14%, Black 6%, Hispanic 8%, Hawaiian/Pacific Islander less than 1%, White 57%, Multi-race 4%, Unknown ethnicity 12%.

The current President of Yale is Richard Levin who received a B.A. from Stanford, B. of Letters from Oxford, and a Ph.D. from Yale. Other notable former Presidents were Reverend Abraham Pierson, the first President, Reverend Timothy Dwight, and A(ngelo) Bartlett Giamatti.

There are many distinguished Yale alumni. Among them are former U.S. Presidents George H.W. Bush, George W. Bush, William "Bill" Clinton, Gerald Ford, and William H. Taft. Also included in the list of notable alumni are Secretary of State Hillary Rodham Clinton, former Secretary of State Cyrus Vance, Massachusetts Senator John Kerry, Connecticut Senator Joseph Liebermann, and General and Ambassador Douglas MacArthur.

http://www.yale.edu/about/, 11/18/11.

www.library.yale.edu/mssa/YHO/presidents.html, 11/18/11.

I discovered the following information about the next Ivy League school—UPenn.

The University of Pennsylvania in Philadelphia, Pennsylvania: Benjamin Franklin, an inventor, writer, ambassador, statesman, and signer of the United States Declaration of Independence founded the University of Pennsylvania in 1740 as a Charity School in Philadelphia. In 1749, Benjamin Franklin organized the Academy of Philadelphia. In 1750, the institutional structure of the Academy and Charitable School was formalized. The Academy and Charitable School opened in 1751. In 1757, the first college class graduated from the Academy and Charitable School.

Currently, Penn (as it is called) has more than 20,000 students at the undergraduate and graduate levels, and twelve graduate and professional schools. The current President is Amy Gutman who received bachelor's and doctor's degrees from Harvard. Notable former Presidents include Judith Rodin and Martin Meyerson. Penn students and graduates have served in many capacities in public and government service, and there are many notable alumni. Included are C.

Everett Koop, former Surgeon General of the United States; William Brennan, Jr., U.S. Supreme Court Justice; and U.S. President William Henry Harrison was a Penn Medical student who did not graduate. Donald Trump of real estate fame is a graduate of the Wharton Business School at Penn.

www.upenn.edu/about/heritage.php, 11/19/11. http://www.upenn.edu/president/meet-president/biography, 11/19/11. and www.archives.upenn.edu/people/notables/political/pennincongressac.html, 11/19/11.

Princeton University in Princeton, New Jersey: Princeton University was chartered in 1746 as the College of New Jersey. It held its first commencement in 1748 with six undergraduate degrees awarded. Princeton had several locations before moving to its present location of Princeton, New Jersey in 1756. The college became a university in 1896 and established the graduate school in 1900. Princeton admitted its first black undergraduates in 1942 and became coeducational in

1969. In 1964, the university awarded its first Ph.D. to a woman.

The undergraduate enrollment is almost 50%–50% between male and females in 2010-2011 with males having a very slight lead. By ethnicity, the undergraduate enrollment for 2010-2011 is as follows: White 48.7%, Black 7.5%, Hispanic 9%, Native American .3%, Asian American 16.9%, Multi-race 3.6%, Pacific Islander .1%, International 10.6%, and Unknown ethnicity 3.3%.

In the graduate schools for 2010-2011, there were 1604 males and 978 females. By ethnicity, the graduate enrollment was as follows: White 40.7%, Black 2.8%, Hispanic 3.2%, Native American .2%, Asian American 6%, Multi-racial 1.4%, Pacific Islander 0%, International 37.1%, Unknown ethnicity 8.6%.

The current President is Shirley M. Tilghman, a Canadian native who earned her Ph.D. in Biochemistry at Temple University in Pennsylvania. Notable former Princeton Presidents are Aaron Burr, Sr., and Woodrow

Wilson who also became President of the United States.

www.princeton.edu/main/about/history/glance/, 11/19/11

Columbia University in New York, New York: I gleaned the following information about Columbia, which was founded in 1754 as King's College by royal charter of King George II of England. Classes started with eight students, and the medical school began in 1767 and was the first to grant the M.D. degree. In 1776, classes halted because of the American Revolution, but they resumed in 1784 under the name Columbia. The law school opened in 1858, and Columbia awarded its first Ph.D. in 1875.

The total undergraduate and graduate enrollment as of Fall 2010 shows that there were 27,606 students at Columbia University, with 50.8% of them women. Of this total, 7934 were undergraduates, with 52.3% of undergraduates women. By ethnicity, Columbia as a whole has 35.1% minorities and 23% non-resident aliens. The undergraduate schools had 45.4% minority enrollment and 11.5% non-resident aliens. The university had 3634 full-time faculty in 2010.

The current President is Lee C. Bollinger, a law school graduate of Columbia and former professor, dean of Law and President of the University of Michigan. Notable alumni include John Jay, first Chief Justice of the U.S. Supreme Court; Alexander Hamilton, first Secretary of the U.S. Treasury; and Gouverneur Morris, author of the final draft of the U.S. Constitution.

www.columbia.edu/content/history.html, 11/19/11

Brown University in Providence, Rhode Island: Brown University is the seventh-oldest college in the United States. It was founded in 1764 at Warren, Rhode Island and called the College of Rhode Island. It relocated to Providence, Rhode Island in 1770. The college was named Brown University in 1804 after Nicholas Brown who gave the college $5000. Brown University admitted women for the first time in 1891. It issued its first master's degree in 1888 and its doctorate in 1889.

Brown was named as the #1 College in America for happiest students. As of Fall 2010, Brown enrolled 6316 undergraduate students, 1923 graduate students, and 410 medical students for a total of 8649 students. The university has 682 full-time faculty. Brown University is the only member of the Ivy League colleges and universities that has an African-American woman as President. Her name is Ruth J. Simmons and she is the 18th President of Brown University, a position she has held since 2001. Simmons graduated Dillard University in New Orleans, Louisiana, an Historically Black College and University. She received her Ph.D. from Harvard University in Romance Languages and Literature in 1973. Dr. Simmons is a former Associate Dean of the Graduate School at the University of Southern California, Provost of Spellman College, Vice Provost of Princeton University, and President of Smith College before becoming President of Brown University.

Notable former Presidents include James Manning, the first President and E.

Gordon Gee, the immediate predecessor of Dr. Simmons.

www.brown.edu/about/history, 11/19/11

Dartmouth College in Hanover, New Hampshire: Dartmouth College is the ninth-oldest college in the United States. It began in 1769 when the Reverend Eleazar Wheelock established it. The college was named for William Legge, the second Earl of Dartmouth, a supporter of Reverend Wheelock's efforts to establish a college. Dartmouth established the medical school in 1797, the nation's first professional school of engineering in 1867, and the first school of management in the world.

As of Fall 2010, the college had 4248 (2143 men, 2105 women) undergraduates and 1893 (1099 men, 794 women) graduate students for a total of 6141 students. The undergraduates are almost 50%–50% between male and female students. There are slightly more men than women among graduate students.

By ethnicity, 35% of undergraduates are of color and 15% of graduate students are of color. There are 8% International students who are undergraduates and 29% International graduate students. Dartmouth has 608 tenured or tenure-track faculty members out of a total of 1004 faculty. The endowment is $3.413 billion as of June 2011..

The current President is Jim Yong Kim who moved from South Korea to the United States at age five. President Kim received his bachelor's degree from Brown University, and his M.D. and Ph.D. from Harvard University in 1991 and 1993 respectively. Ten years later Kim received the coveted MacArthur "genius" Award. He worked at the Harvard Medical School and the World Health Organization before becoming President of Dartmouth. Perhaps the most famous Dartmouth alumnus is Daniel Webster.

www.dartmouth.edu/home/about/facts. html, 11/19/11.

Cornell University in Ithaca, New York: Cornell was founded in 1865 by Ezra Cornell and Andrew Dickson White. It opened in 1868. As of 2009-2010, the university has approximately 2800 faculty members, and the student enrollment is almost 22,000, with 13,931 of those undergraduates. By gender and ethnicity, undergraduates are 31% minority and 51% male to 49% female. Graduate and Professional students range from 15% to 30% minority students based on location of graduate/professional student facilities, whether in Ithaca or New York City. The overall ratio of men to women is approximately 51% to 52% male and 48% to 49% female.

The current President is David J. Skorton who received B.A. and M.D. degrees from Northwestern University in 1970 and 1974, respectively.

www.cornell.edu/about/, 11/19/11.

Overall, the admission rate to the Ivy League is low and the graduation rates are high. *U.S. News and World Reports* list the following data for 2011 for admission and graduation.

The Ivy League Colleges and Universities

Brown University admitted 13.5% with graduation rate of 86%. Cornell University admitted 20.5% of applicants and graduated 85% of students in four years. Columbia University admitted 10.4% with graduation rate of 87%. Dartmouth College admitted 15.3% of applicants and graduated 85% of students in four years. Harvard University admitted 9% of applicants and the four-year graduation rate was 88%. Princeton University admitted 9.5% of applicants and graduated 90% of students in four years. The University of Pennsylvania admitted 15.9% of applicants and graduated 88% of students, and Yale University admitted 9.6% of applicants and graduated 90% of students in four years.

In previous years, the graduation rates for Harvard and some of the other Ivies was as high as 97% of students in a four-year period. Then or now, it is obvious that in the Ivy League, admission rates are low and graduation rates are high.

The reputation for success is unsurpassed in the Ivy League. Indeed many prospective students put forth great effort to apply to and secure admission to one or more of these venerable institutions. What effect they actually have on an individual's career is not easily measured, but it is thought that an Ivy League education automatically catapults a person to a higher rung on the ladder, a higher degree of success, and a lifetime of fulfilled promises. Of course the last statement about a lifetime of fulfilled promises is a bit far-fetched. The data show some things that can be measured. For example, Greg Mankiws in his blog on September 18, 2006 reports that about 10% of CEOs heading the top 500 companies received undergraduate degrees from Ivy League colleges. Of the 10% Ivy degrees, Harvard presented the most CEOs. While 10% is low, it is not so bad when put into context. You see, only about 1% of graduates in the United States have Ivy degrees, yet they hold 10% of the top 500 CEO positions. In context, that means that an Ivy graduate is 10 times more likely to become a CEO than other college graduates.

Certainly the question, Do Ivy League alumni make better CEOs? is an appropriate one to ask. In *Management Issues* on September 20, 2010, Brian Bolton of the University of New Hampshire and co-authors Sanjai Bhagat of the University of Colorado at Boulder, and Ajay Subramanian of Georgia State University found the answer to that question to be "No." They say that a degree from a top-ranking university does not affect a company's long-term performance. The authors examined more than 2600 cases of CEO turnover from 1992 to 2007 to conduct their study and reach their conclusions. Perhaps boards and researchers should not place so much emphasis on an individual's education when trying to find a leader who will lead the company well for employees and shareholders. They should rely on other factors such as experience and results along with education. But what an individual who is interested in the Ivy League has to consider is what does and Ivy League education mean to him or her? If an individual is fortunate enough to go through the admission process at one of those eight schools and gain admission status, it seems inconceivable to turn an Ivy League school down. It is true that an Ivy League education is expensive, but it is worth it to most people. There are colleges and universities that are more expensive than the Ivy League and an Ivy League education is no more expensive than a house, a luxury car, and a closet full of expensive clothes and shoes, if you want to look at it that way. An education that helps to launch your career and future for you and your family for years to come is much more valuable than a Cadillac Escalade, a Jaguar, or a Mercedes Benz. Any two of those for a two-car family would cost almost the same as four years in the Ivy League and will not last an entire career as that degree will. It comes down to an individual's value system and what is most important in his or her life at the time.

I would say that, as an Ivy League graduate, my joy and elation in being admitted to an institution that rejects 90% to 92% of its applicants worldwide matched my feeling of self-esteem and fulfillment I felt at being able to matriculate successfully through the program and the pride of accomplishment I felt to graduate with two graduate degrees – master's and doctor's—from a prestigious and renowned three and a half centuries-old institution of higher learning. To sit where so many world leaders, Nobel Prize and Pulitzer Prize winners have sat is a boost to my ego and confidence and in my ability to go out and lead others and make a difference and contribution while doing so. Additionally, there are many powerful friends that I was able to cultivate along the way. This is not limited to just Ivy colleges and universities, but it is certainly true of them.

The Ivy League creates an atmosphere of confidence and competence. They never tire of assuring their students that they are bright, capable, shapers of the future, and I as a student never tired of hearing it and believing it. It makes for a self-fulfilling prophesy that reflects well on the Ivies when their graduates go out believing they are great, can do great things, and actually do those things they set out to achieve. The universities' credentials and reputations make their graduates look good, and, in turn, their graduates' accomplishments reflect well upon the Ivy League and further enhance their reputation and mystique.

# Resources

About Brown. Brown University. 19 Nov. 2011. *<http://www.brown.edu/about/history>*.

About Columbia. Columbia University. 19 Nov. 2011. *<http://www.columbia.edu/content/history.html>*.

About Cornell. Cornell University. 19 Nov. 2011. <http://www.cornell.edu/about/>.

About Harvard. "Harvard At A Glance," Harvard University. 18 Nov. 2011. <http://www.harvard.edu/harvard-glance>.

About Harvard. "Harvard At A Glance," Harvard University. 18 Nov. 2011. <http://www.harvard.edu/history/>.

About Harvard. "Harvard At A Glance," Harvard University. 18 Nov. 2011. *<http://www.harvard.edu/history-presidency>*.

About Princeton. Princeton University. 19 Nov. 2011. *<http://www.princeton.edu/main/about/history/glance/>*.

About Penn. University of Pennsylvania. 19 Nov. 2011. *<www.upenn.edu/about/heritage.php>*.

About Penn. University of Pennsylvania. 19 Nov. 2011. *<http://www.upenn.edu/president/meet-president/biography>*.

About Penn. University of Pennsylvania. 19 Nov. 2011. *<http://www.archives.upenn.edu/people/notables/political/pennincongressac.html>*.

About Yale. Yale University. 18 Nov. 2011. *<http://www.yale.edu/about/>*.

About Yale. Yale University. 18 Nov. 2011. *<http://www.library.yale.edu/mssa/YHO/presidents.html>*.

Bolton, Brian, et al. *"Do Ivy League Alumni Make Better CEOs?,"* Management Issues. 20 Sept. 2010. Accessed 18 Nov. 2011.

*Graduation Rates in Ivy League Schools.* U.S. News and World Reports. 2011.

Mankiws, Greg. *"Ivy League CEOs."* Greg Mankiws Blog. 18 Sept. 2006. Accessed 18 Nov. 2011. *<www.gregmankiw.blogspot. com/2006_09_01_archive.html>.*

The Woodrow Wilson National Fellowship Foundation. *www.woodrow.org/about_fellows/ index.php, 11/18/11.*

www.ingramcontent.com/pod-product-compliance
Lightning Source LLC
Chambersburg PA
CBHW060514100426
42743CB00009B/1308